Here is hilarious, yet sound guidance on how to let a house virtually clean itself. Hundreds of sensible suggestions for the harried homemaker, from tips on handling electrical equipment to care of clothes and entertaining. The very useful and funny contents include **Don't Just Do Something, Sit There** and **Stains, Spots, Blots, Scars and Dueling Wounds.**

Other Fawcett Crest Books by Peg Bracken:

The I Hate to Cook Book
I Try to Behave Myself (forthcoming)

The
I Hate to Housekeep
Book

PEG BRACKEN

DRAWINGS BY HILARY KNIGHT

A FAWCETT CREST BOOK

Fawcett Publications, Inc., Greenwich, Conn.
Member of American Book Publishers Council, Inc.

A Fawcett Crest Book published by arrangement with
Harcourt, Brace & World, Inc.

This book contains the complete text of the original hardcover edition.

Library of Congress Catalog Card Number: 62-16729

PRINTING HISTORY
Harcourt, Brace & World edition published September 26, 1962
First printing, July 1962
Second printing, October 1962
Third printing, December 1962
Fourth printing, June 1963
Fifth printing, July 1964
Sixth printing, January 1965
A dual selection of the Better Homes & Gardens Family
Book Shelf, July 1964

First Fawcett Crest printing, July 1965
Second printing, August 1965
Third printing, October 1965
Fourth printing, December 1965

Published by Fawcett World Library,
67 West 44th Street, New York, N. Y. 10036
Printed in the United States of America

Dedicated,
for many a good and sufficient reason,
to
Ruth Bracken,
with love

Acknowledgments are gratefully made to Mary McClintock Bosch and to Mary Jane Waldo, for their valuable assistance; and to the authors and publishers who have given their permission to reproduce copyright material, as follows: Peter de Vries, *The Tents of Wickedness,* © 1960, Little, Brown and Company; Lillian Rogers Parks and Frances Spatz Leighton, *My Thirty Years Backstairs at the White House,* © 1961, Fleet Publishing Corporation; Christopher Fry, *The Lady's Not for Burning,* copyright 1950, Oxford University Press; *Gourmet Magazine,* for the poem "Evolution" by Peg Bracken, copyright 1949; and, for lines from *Mine the Harvest* by Edna St. Vincent Millay, Harper & Row, copyright 1954 by Norma Millay Ellis.

P. B.

Foreword

For a number of long years, through no fault of my own, I have been shin-deep in the business of giving advice on Housewifery. This is a better name for it, I think, than Homemaking, which is rather too pretty, like Nuisance Abatement Officer for Dogcatcher. Housewifery is more honest and more inclusive.

Housewifery isn't among the Seven Lively Arts, though it can certainly be regarded as the Eighth. It is lively indeed, in the same way sand-hogging is. They both take courage, muscle, and endurance. The main difference between a sand hog and a housewife is that he has a nice clean tunnel later to show for his efforts, and it stays put, while she has it all to do over again the next day. She must simply keep tunneling.

She is faced constantly with mute but persistent supplicants for attention. There are several choices; move it, clean it, shine it, brush it, wash it. Or hide it.

I have been doing all this by myself for about twenty years, and I find it hard on the manicure. I've found, too, that none of the books about it does me much good. The household experts hand out cures that are worse than the ailment. They expect you to do things that depress you merely to think about, let alone do. They think you'll actually keep an orderly file of all the washing instructions that come with the family clothes, once you've been told to. The efficiently organized expert makes the mistake of assuming that you, too, want to be one.

My own goals are more modest. I only want to make it around the clock, that's all, and I don't want to think about it too much, either, because I'm thinking about something else. If you're a bit nervous in the service anyway, and your mind is on raising the African violet or running an office or painting a picture, reorganizing yourself into an efficient housewife is a giant step you're not about to take. You want an aspirin, not radical surgery.

So, though I admit hastily and gratefully that many of the things in this book were discovered or invented by experts (even the experts slip up once in a while and recommend something you'd consider doing), just as many of them weren't.

Indeed, some of the wee nuggets herein are ones that I mined, all by myself.

Take the matter of diapers. I had often heard, from wiser folk than I, that a soft, old, much-laundered diaper makes as nice a dish towel as any girl could want. When my child outgrew the diaper stage, I learned that this was true.

However, as one runs out of babies, one tends to run out of diapers. This happened to me, and for at least three months I was wiping the dishes on anything handy. Then, one day, with the lightning-swift grasp of fundamentals that has marked my slightest move in the household arts, I realized that *you don't have to have another baby in order to buy more diapers.* You just go buy some, that's all. If you don't have a wedding ring, let alone a baby, and if this sort of thing bothers you, you can always have the diapers gift-wrapped.

A note, here, about language. I suppose it was inevitable that around so old a business as housekeeping—surely the second-oldest profession—a special vocabulary should have evolved.

It has. All the housekeeping experts say "food preparation area" when they mean "kitchen," and "soiled spots" when they mean "dirty places," and so forth.

In this book I prefer to call things by their right names, if they will let me. (Sometimes they don't let you. Once, when I wrote a book about having a baby, I wanted to use the word "pain," having come to a point in the proceedings where that seemed to be the only word that said what I meant. But they changed it to "discomfort." These are things the writer can't do a thing about, and he shouldn't be blamed for them.)

One more point: the housewifery manuals I have seen pay little attention to certain aspects I consider pertinent; for instance, how to make yourself do things you don't like to do, and how to remember to do them. Some of these techniques are included here. There are some swift recipes, too, for days when you shouldn't have got up in the first place but still must go that last long mile and cook dinner. And there are some slightly slower recipes for company. And there is the matter of keeping up a good front—

Indeed, there is a small mountain of miscellany here—and naturally enough, in a book about the most miscellaneous of all miscellaneous businesses. Putting the scraps together was like sorting confetti in a wind tunnel, and you should have seen the ones that blew away. Catch them as they sail past, if you can. And meanwhile, here are the rest, in a book by a nonexpert for nonexperts, with warm good wishes, and best of luck to the African violet.

Peg Bracken

Contents

1: Mousing Around the House

" 'Oh, it's too bad!' she cried.
'I never saw such a house for getting in the way!
Never!' "

—THROUGH THE LOOKING-GLASS

THERE ARE three kinds of housekeepers. There is the spotless housekeeper, who won't stop, and there is the spotful housekeeper, who won't start. Then there is the occasional or random housekeeper, whose book this is.

The random housekeeper is the girl who spoils her manicure tearing the top off a box of soap chips just before she sees the OPEN HERE in large letters over the spout. She sets her automatic oven with a sure touch—the time it is to start cooking and the time it is to stop cooking—then forgets to

13

put the food in. (The Rh factor is one which neither the packaging people nor the manufacturers have so far been able to lick.) And she uses her dust mop periodically, when the planets are in their proper configurations and when she can remember where she left it the last time.

Her heart is in the right place, but she is an impulsive little thing, that's all, and when it comes to housekeeping, she'd rather be doing nearly anything else, and she generally is.

Also, unlike the spotless housekeeper, she gets pretty tired of the scutwork involved, to use the good old Navy term for chores that any boob can do, like cleaning up after people. The longer you stay with housekeeping, the more you begin to feel like one of those elderly gentlemen who creeps around the park, picking up gum wrappers and butts with a nail on the end of a stick, except that he gets more fresh air.

Consider, for a moment, your spotless housekeeper. She housekeeps most of the time, apportioning various chores to different days: Tuesday morning is ironing morning. She calls this Not Letting the House Get Away from Her, making it sound a little like a nervous filly.

But the occasional housekeeper doesn't know she'll be ironing that day, nor does she care to. It would depress her to know that this was the shape and color of next Tuesday morning. She would rather just let it happen, should an ill-natured Providence so decree.

In fact, the spotless housekeeper even housekeeps while she cooks. She can put dinner for eight on the table, and you'd never know anything had been happening in the kitchen. But she loses out on a lot of good talk this way, and there's not much point to it. After all, you expect to see a few bodies lying around a battlefield. When you cook, you cook. When you clean, you clean. Sufficient unto the time is the evil thereof.

In other areas, too, the spotless housekeeper behaves oddly. I know one whose living-room furniture will shortly be as many-layered as an onion. She slip-covered her upholstery, which, she felt, was too pretty to sit on. But then so were the slip covers, and she felt she had to protect *them,* with taut plastic casings. Now she has discovered that a small cigarette spark makes a big hole in the plastic, and I don't know what she's going to cover the plastic with, but I'm sure she'll think of something.

Right here is as good a place as any for the first of five important reminders:

1. *Don't cover things up unless it's absolutely necessary. It just means you'll have two things to take care of and keep clean instead of one.*

For example, don't throw a throw rug on the kitchen floor in front of the sink or the stove (or in the bathroom either). The reason you picked linoleum or vinyl instead of wall-to-wall carpeting was so you could wipe it up, remember? And it's easier to wipe up a spatter than wash a rug.

(If you want a small sponge-rubber mat for resting your feet, that's another matter. But if you're going to spend that much time at the sink or the stove, you're probably not a random housekeeper anyway, and you'd do better to pull up a stool and sit down.)

Take pantry shelves. Don't put anything on them except groceries. If they're enameled or shellacked or varnished, leave them alone. If you inherit some stained ugly ones, and they bother you, then cover them permanently with self-sticking paper. Never use anything loose, because presently it will need dusting or wiping off, and so will the shelf you put it on.

Or take so simple an object as a toaster. Leave it un-tea-cozied, and if somebody gives you a cover for it, give it to somebody else. A toaster cover will get dusty and sticky, and you'll have to wash it or wipe it, in addition to polishing your toaster—which you'll have to do anyway, what with crumbs and buttery fingers and one thing and another.

People who say dust will get into your toaster are just being silly. I never made a piece of dusty toast in my life. If you're going to start this sort of thing, you'll find yourself making wee dust covers for the glass in your bathroom toothbrush holder, one for each day in the week, and goodness only knows where it's apt to end.

Really, one of the few things it's sensible to cover is chair arms and sofa arms. The usual way is with removable rectangles of the slip-cover or upholstery fabric. But I know a lady who didn't have any extra material and used Irish linen place mats, and they look fine.

2. *Keep the pots and pans you cook in out of sight, in the cupboards or drawers.*

The only people who should hang up their copper cooking pots are those who enjoy polishing pot bottoms. For you must polish them nearly every time you use them or they'll look terrible, which makes as much sense as washing the tires every time you drive the car.

There is a lot of confusion around, these days, about what is an *objet d'art* and what isn't. Log-cabin ladies hung their cooking equipment handy because they used it most of the time. There was no other place to put it anyway, and it made a bright spot in the dark cabin.

But think of the pretties we have today! Copper pots and pans are no better looking than a lot of other things that don't need polishing, and the freewheeling housewife will do well to keep this in mind. The quaint copper colander I saw in an antique shop yesterday is still just a round object full of holes, and a pan's a pan for a' that.

You'll do far better to hang up a picture you like—your favorite Dufy print, perhaps, or White Rock's Lady of the Lake,* for that matter—whatever makes you feel good when you look at it. In the housekeeping game you need all the sunshine you can get. And if you feel that you simply *must* hang up a pot, then hang up a bright enameled-iron one that you merely wipe off.

3. *Each time you give the house a good going-over, start with a different room.*

It is quite likely that you'll peter out, you know, after a few hours' slogging, and this rule insures that you will at least peter out in a different place each time. (If you stopped in the *same* place, year after year, for instance just before you got to the back bedroom, you would eventually have to saw it off.)

4. *Establish a clutter depot.*

There are two kinds of clutter.

* And have them framed with nonglare glass, so the kitchen light can't trip you up.

There is artful clutter, as seen in full-color magazine pictures: the nice old calfbound First Folio Shakespeare face down on the nice old French fruitwood love seat with the white kid opera gloves hanging down the back.

Then there is honest clutter, as exemplified by the ski-sock on the mantel and the gas bill on the television set, and all the other odd things which somebody should have put away and didn't.

It is this latter type of clutter to which you, as a random housewife, are especially prone.

If you don't remove the out-of-place object the first time you notice it, it may well hang around for months. Because your mind is so often elsewhere as you gaze about your familiar domain, the ski-sock or the gas bill quickly becomes part of the accustomed scenery, and you don't see it any more.

Therefore it is important to establish one central place— an otherwise unused closet, chest, or drawer—where all these things go. This enables you to make a clean sweep, on those mornings when you feel up to it and are willing to concentrate.

Then it is up to each person in the house to rescue his own belongings. If he doesn't see it around, he knows where to look. And if, in addition, everyone has *one* inviolate place he may keep as messy as he wants—for we all need one, just as we all need an occasional solitary moment in which to stamp and scream—he needn't feel too put upon.

5. *Act immediately on whatever housewifely impulses come your way.*

Being but destiny's plaything, you must seize upon the moment when you notice that something needs doing, and *do* it, with whatever you have at hand to do it with.

Say, for instance, that you notice a little jam on the woodwork. Now, this curiously specialized age of ours has produced a specific cleaner or polisher for anything you care to name. With this in the back of her mind, the random housewife tends to rationalize herself out of wiping the jam off the woodwork until she gets a box of that new woodwork stuff she was hearing about, at which improbable time (she thinks grandly) she'll do all the woodwork in the whole house.

However, a damp dishrag or a sponge rubbed on a simple cake of wet soap will help a great deal in this situation, and in a lot of other situations too.

To sum up: forget the old cliché to the effect that anything worth doing is worth doing well. This isn't true. When you're going at a high lope, a fast swipe at the sink is a lot better than no swipe at all.

But back to the spotless housekeeper.

The truth is—and you must remember this—*you don't want to be one*, even though you may have an occasional qualm as you watch the pile of unironed clothes rising like bread dough. The question you must ask yourself at these times is this:

Who, or whom, are you keeping house FOR?

Certainly not for your friends and neighbors. If their windows are shinier than yours are, it will make them feel all warm inside, and they'll like you for it. You never heard a woman say, "I simply adore Marcia, she's the most *meticulous* housekeeper!"

Certainly not for your children. You don't keep house for them, but in spite of them.

No, what you keep house for is for you and your husband, but mainly for you. Because if things get too cluttered, you won't be able to think straight, and you never *will* get past record two in your Conversational French course.

Husbands, with a few grim exceptions, don't care much. They want a modest modicum of order, that's all. They'd rather not see how it got there, either, and they hate the whine of a vacuum cleaner only slightly less than the wail of a policeman's siren hard behind.

This modest modicum, then, is the thing to keep in mind. And don't let it be upgraded too far by other housekeepers. Remember, women have a tendency to grow neater as they grow older anyway. In spite of yourself, you can turn into a compulsive picture-straightener, shade-twitcher, and ashtray-emptier, which is a straight shoot to a terribly nervous old age.

One more word, before we press on: never think unkindly about someone else's housekeeping, nor speak unkindly either.

You don't know what she may be up against. Perhaps she gets dizzy spells whenever she thinks about woodwork. And don't be too critical if you consider her too neat. Perhaps you don't really know her husband. Perhaps she married one of those grim exceptions, and maybe little Napoleon turns purple if the window blind is one quarter inch out of line.

There are many things we can't know, that's all, and inasmuch as we all have our troubles, it behooves us all to hold our tongues.

As Herman Melville has put it so aptly, ". . . everybody else is one way or the other served in much the same way—either in a physical or metaphysical point of view, that is; and so the universal thump is passed around, and all hands should rub each other's shoulder blades and be content."

2: The Bride's Own ABC's

"Sally go round the sun
Sally go round the moon
Sally go round the chimney pots
On a Saturday afternoon."

—MOTHER GOOSE

A is for Alphabet

THE ALPHABET is a handy thing to have around the house.

For instance, you can organize your canned goods with it, Applesauce to Zucchini.

Also whatever is in the medicine cabinet, Aspirin to Zinc Ointment.

Also your herbs and spices, Allspice to Thyme.

You may organize your books alphabetically too—by Author, if you mainly remember authors, or by Title or by Subject. Or perhaps you remember books by their color, as a friend of mine does.

She thinks, "Oh, yes, that pink book, by what's-his-name. . . ." So she keeps all like-colored books together, which results in some improbable shelfmates, with *The Rubaiyat* next to *The Complete Dog Book*. It works for her, though, and the blocks of color are pretty.

And you can use the alphabet as an inexpensive tranquilizer. When you can't sleep, try a Minister's Cat: the minister's cat is an Ardent cat who Adores Angoras. A Bellicose cat who Beats up Bulldogs. A Charming cat who Cuts Capers. And so on, around and around, until you fall asleep or it's time to get up.

B is for Burn Ointment

Always keep it near the stove, not in the bathroom medicine cabinet, because who ever gets burned in the bathroom?

C is for Code

You and your husband had better establish one quickly, for getting yourselves out of miserable situations.

This is easily done with names. If he usually calls you Sue but suddenly, in company, calls you Sweetie, this means he can't stand any more home movies, and you'd better rescue him with a resounding lie, like a resounding headache. (And, if you ordinarily call him Herb but suddenly call him Darling, he can consider himself similarly alerted.)

A code, or firm rule, will minimize future marital disasters, too, such as the inevitable occasions when you'll lose each other at airports or department stores. You must decide between you, now, who is to stay put and who is to hunt (it's usually better that he does, because he isn't wearing high heels).

And you must fix upon one sure, permanent place at home for leaving messages: on a bulletin board, or a mantel, or under one particular clock.

I know a wife who decided she was tired of both housekeeping and husband and determined to leave them. She left a letter somewhere, but he didn't find it. When she came back the next day to pick up a few things, he was understandably puzzled and so was she, because she couldn't remember, for the life of her, where she'd put it. They became so engrossed in looking for the letter that they got quite friendly again, and they're still married.

So you see what can happen.

D is for Dripping Faucets

A dripping cold-water faucet merely stains the porcelain and ruins the nervous system. But a dripping *hot*-water faucet costs you money. It can amount to as much as eight or ten extra dollars a month on your gas or electric bill. Therefore you must take up this situation immediately with your husband or handyman, because there are more interesting ways to spend eight or ten dollars.

E is for Equipment

Once you've acquired the basic biggish things for cleaning, washing, and cooking, proceed as porcupines are said to make love: quite carefully. Otherwise you'll be up to your bride's bouquet in unused electric bottle washers and corn shuckers. I am personally acquainted with two food liquefiers which made just two frozen Daiquiris apiece before they were retired to the top shelf of the pantry.

Borrow the gadget first, if you can. Swap something for a week, in return for your sister-in-law's deep-fat fryer, to find out if you'd really use it if you had one. *Because maybe you wouldn't.* And when you buy everything in sight, you feel overworked if you use it all and guilty if you don't.

Think of the attachments attachable to any self-respecting modern vacuum cleaner! At least six, not counting the paint sprayer, all of which you are privileged to use before you drag out the wax applicator and the floor polisher. But Great-Grandma just moved gently around behind her broom for a while, then laid the dust with the polish-soaked dustcloth she fished out of her Mason jar, and had time to sit down to read *Love or Lechery: The Story of a Good Girl's Temptation,* and a rattling good story it was, too.

F is for Flour

Sift your flour from the flour sack right into your flour canister. If it doesn't get bounced around, and there is no reason it should, it will sit there lightly, and you won't need to sift again when you bake. Just measure.

G is for Gliders

Chairs with little pointy legs dimple your floors just as spike heels do. Should you happen to have a chair of this type, you might suggest to your husband that he hoist his big handsome self out of it just long enough to put some wider gliders or rubber pads on its feet.

H is for Hard-boiled Eggs

You are supposed to say "hard-cooked," but I have never noticed much difference if they've boiled for a while.

To discourage their cracking, salt the water heavily. Or prick them with a needle before you put them into the water, and start them in cold water, not hot.

Sometimes you'll run into an infuriating hard-boiled egg with a glued-on shell, which must be chipped away bit by bit, and the end result looks pock-marked. To prevent this, plunge your hard-boiled eggs into cold water the instant they leave the hot.

I is for Instant Housekeeping

This is for those occasions when you're going to be out of the house all day, but you don't want the house to look like it when your husband gets home.

Therefore, the minute he leaves in the morning, you steam into your Instant Housekeeping, which is usually housekeeping backward. Patterns vary, according to the focal point of your house and the habits and peculiarities of your spouse.

For instance, your own crash-plan might be:
1. Set the table for dinner
2. Build a modest pitcher of Martinis and set it in the refrigerator

3. Lay a fire
4. Throw out the dead flowers
5. Shut all the closet doors and cupboard drawers
6. Do the breakfast dishes
7. Make the bed.

Then you can sweep, dust, and all that sort of thing, if there's still time. But remember: when life is rich and full, and the chips are you know where, do *last* things *first.*

J is for silver or gold Jewelry

Shine it with toothpaste,* using an old soft toothbrush.

K is for Kilowatt

This is an electrical term. I visualize a kilowatt as small and round and black, like a peppercorn, though I have never seen one.

However, you buy electricity by the *kilowatt-hour,* just as you buy sugar by the pound. It's a good idea to call up your electric company and find out what you pay for one in your community. Then you know whether you can afford to forget to turn the oven off, or leave your light bulbs burning.

For instance, where I live, kilowatt-hours are a real bargain. They cost only a penny apiece. This means I can burn a 100-watt light bulb for ten hours for a penny, or around 70¢ a month.

Also—and I asked the man very particularly about this—it costs me approximately 38¢ to leave the oven on, at 350°, all night. (That is with the oven door shut. If the oven door is open, and the oven is blasting away all night at 350°, it would cost me twice that.)

So, as you can see, even in a place where electricity is cheap, you might as well burn up dollar bills as try to heat your kitchen with the oven. And in your town, things might be much worse, if you don't have some nice big dams around to furnish hydroelectric power. You might even be paying as much as 7¢ for each and every kilowatt-hour you buy. This would cost you 7¢ to burn one 100-

---

* In fact, you can use it on any sort of metal—it's just gentler than most copper and brass polishes, and takes more rubbing.

watt light bulb for ten hours, or about $5.10 if you left it on all month.

So find out.

L is for Luxurious Groceries

The most painless way to buy these things—artichoke hearts, French-fried almonds, smoked sturgeon, and so forth—is to include one in each strictly utilitarian load of groceries—soap powder, peanut butter, and that sort of thing. Somehow the cost tends to get lost in the cost of the practical items, and this lessens the sting. It's all a matter of self-deception, and you can do it if you try.

M is for Marketing in General

You will probably become confused, as most people do, about box sizes: the Jumbo, the King size, the Mammoth, and the Large Family Economy. Indeed, many customers would welcome a size called the Little Gyppo, for here, at least, they would know where they stood. Certain box sizes might well be called the Big Gyppo anyway, for they contain not an ounce more than two ordinary ones, at exactly twice the price. You're stuck, in addition, with a great clumsy box that's too tall for your shelf.

Some people have been known to take slide rules to market, and compute. You might do this if you have one and know how to use it.

If you don't, figure it out on the back of your grocery list. If the big clumsy box *still* is a good bargain, you might as well buy it. You can always repackage it yourself. Funnel the soap flakes or whatever into old empty quart Mason jars or square-sided gin bottles, which will use your space more economically.

Otherwise, just choose according to which product you like, or which set of plastic tumblers you are completing at the time.

Remember, too: some seemingly hopeless boxes will go on your shelf if you lay them on their sides.

N is for Nylons

You may freeze new nylon stockings in water, in your

ice-cube trays with the dividers removed, then let them thaw
naturally, then squeeze them out and let them dry.

People who do this swear that the stockings will then wear
about three times longer. However, this doesn't prevent
snags. In my own case, I'd have to freeze a couple of active
kittens too, to do any real good, and I wouldn't dream of it.

O is for Odds and Ends

OVENS. Never leave leftover biscuits in the oven, because
you'll forget they're there and burn them up, sure as you're
born, next time you turn on the oven. (There is more
about Ovens on page 76. There is more about Biscuits on
page 160.)

OLDE ENGLYSSHE COUGHE SIROP. This will charm the socks off
any husband coming down with a cold; and if you can get
the rest of his clothes off too, and get him into bed, he will
have a good night's sleep, with no coughing.

> Fill a cheese glass ⅓ full with black currant jam.
> Add 2 ounces of bourbon or rye whisky.
> Fill it up with hot water, then stir and serve with solici-
> tude.

OATMEAL. Adding chopped raw apple to hot oatmeal greatly
improves the oatmeal, as nearly anything does, and it doesn't
hurt the apple.

OLD MOUSETRAPS. If you're out of mice, you can still use the
mousetrap. Paint it, if you like, and nail it to the wall,
spring up, to hold your unpaid bills and old love letters.

OMELETS. Your omelets will stand up long enough for you to
sit down if you add a teaspoon of flour per egg.

P is for Plastic Bags

You will thank yourself for buying only bread that comes
in reusable plastic bags and keeping all the bags. (You also
keep them away from little children.) You can use these bags
in 500 different ways. For instance:

Put one on each foot to protect good shoes if you must
cook when you're dressed up
Use them in your dresser drawers as
lingerie cases
glove cases
hosiery cases
handkerchief cases
Freeze dampened clothes in them, when you get tired of
ironing before you've finished
Use them as shoe covers when you travel
Put wet bathing suits and caps in them
Pack food in them for picnics
Slip them over ice-cream cartons to catch drips
Put cookies or leftover muffins in them to freeze
. . . plus 489 other purposes there isn't room to list here.

Q is for Questions

Ask them. You cannot rely on your mother-in-law to
volunteer much information these days. Most mothers-in-
law feel so beat down by the bad publicity they've had that
they'd be afraid to speak up if they saw you peering into
a gas tank by matchlight. But they're grateful for being asked.

So is nearly everyone else. People love to talk about their
specialties, and people love brides anyway.

So ask the butcher (and if you deal at a supermarket, where
the meat is apparently untouched by human hands, ring the
little bell and a butcher will magically appear). Ask the dry
cleaner, ask the plumber, ask the lineoleum man, ask the
motherly-looking lady beside you at the linen counter when
you're buying sheets, ask the baker.

Once I asked the baker what was the best way to reheat
rolls. He said, "For 20 or 30 minutes in a very lukewarm
oven, like 175 or 200." If you do it this way, he continued,
instead of in a 400 oven for 5 minutes, you can continue to
reheat them, meal after meal if you have to, and they'll never
become too crisp and hard. So I tried it and found it true.

R is for Reciprocal Trade Agreements

When you are cooking for two, it's a relief to have a
friend in a similar fix, or find one. Then you can swap
leftovers.

You, for instance, can cook a turkey and she can cook a ham. Then, after a while, you can trade what's left, in some equitable fashion, remembering that the turkey probably cost less than the ham did. You can do this handily with pies, cakes, casseroles, and molded salads too.

S is for Silver

The Grange Lady will tell you that the best way to polish your silver is to use it all the time, but this is one of the half-truths they are so fond of. For instance: "It takes only minutes to wash down your basement walls," but they don't say how many.

The truth is that even though you use it daily, silver won't have that high company gleam. Also, this takes some doing if you possess more silver than family. Anyway, you may like your stainless steel better with your pottery.

Therefore you still must polish your sterling flatware once in a while, or get someone to do it for you.

The easiest way—except for ornate patterns which have darkened backgrounds for contrast—is the aluminum-salt-and-soda way:

> Put a quart of water in a big aluminum saucepan or kettle, and add a tablespoon each of baking soda and salt. Bring this to a boil.
>
> Drop 4 or 5 pieces in at once, and let them boil about 3 minutes. Then fish them out with tongs, wash, rinse, and dry.

(I've heard it suggested that this method may remove some microscopically thin film of silver. But I've seen ardent silver polishers of the silver-cream-and-elbow-grease school who must have removed more than that with each polishing. Thin old spoons are more highly regarded than fat new ones anyway; and in any case, I'm sure my silver will last longer than I will.)

Then, when you're finished, you can wrap individual place settings in pieces of aluminum foil, if you want to and if you don't have a tarnish-proof chest, and put it away.

Don't let any rubber touch your silver or stay in the same drawer with it. It makes ugly black marks.

Don't store salt shakers with salt in them, either.

And save up some small screw-top glass jars to store little things in, like demitasse spoons.

T is for Tea Towels

White ones are best—diapers, flour-sack squares, or white terry cloth—because you can treat them rougher without noticeable harm.

The way to keep a tea towel looking as fresh as the little old lady's down the street is: a) use a clean one every day, and b) when you put them in the washing machine, sprinkle 2 tablespoons of sal soda on them, *then* add your detergent, *then* your water. (This treatment keeps colored tea towels looking fresh, too.)

In excesses of mad enthusiasm, women have been known to boil their tea towels with a lemon rind, to whiten them. But this doesn't do much besides steam up the kitchen. Also, a tea towel that's seen long and honorable service has a right to a few scars and blotches, as don't we all.

(T IS ALSO FOR TOMATO. You'll probably find that a fresh tomato keeps better on the refrigerator shelf than it does in the vegetable compartment.)

U is for Upstairs

If you have one, keep a basket at the foot of the stairway for things that go Up. Keep another at the top for things that go Down. This keeps you from feeling so much like a Tweeny—those little 'tween-stairs maids who inhabit English detective stories and keep pounding up and down the stairs like pistons.

If your stairway is a pretty one, get a good-looking brass or tole bucket or a rattan basket, or whatever fits in.

V is for Vacuum

You can vacuum farther without stopping and stooping to plug it in again elsewhere if you attach a heavy extension cord to the vacuum cord. I have never noticed that this lessens the suction any, although I haven't checked it with anyone because I don't want to spoil my amateur standing.

W is for Waffles

A stuck waffle happens to every woman at least once,

and always at the superbly wrong time, although there *is* no superbly right time for the frustrating mess this results in.

It happens because you let your waffle iron get too hot and/or didn't put enough oil in your waffle batter.

You must get all the old charred waffle out of the grid without using water. Use a table knife and a stiff brush. (If you don't feel like tackling this at the moment, add a little more egg and milk to your batter and have some rather mediocre pancakes instead.) Then oil the grid lightly next time you use it, with a pastry brush, and add an extra tablespoon of oil to your batter. Make sure your iron isn't too hot, and get going.

X is for Xtra

XTRA BLANKETS. If you're minus storage space, a good place to keep extra blankets is right in the bed, under the mattress pad.

XTRA GRAVY. When you cook a turkey, you'll probably need extra gravy before you're done with it. Buy some, by the can or the carton, at your grocer's or at the delicatessen. This will eke out your own and make the turkey easier to face through the weeks to come.

Y is for Yoga

Three years ago, a friend of mine gave a posh luncheon for the Symphony Committee and the conductor. Among other splendid things in the middle of the table were a beautiful fruit salad and a large silver-lidded jar for the curry mayonnaise.

When the guests were seated, and she removed the lid from the mayonnaise pot, there, waving his whiskers, with his tiny paws braced on the rim, was a little gray mouse. He pushed himself up out of the mayonnaise, peered at the people, shook the mayonnaise off his paws, one by one, then jumped smack into the middle of the conductor's plate.

I never heard what happened to the wee, sleekit, mayonnaise-laden beastie. But my friend is all right. When I saw her last week, she was sitting up, and we think she'll be taking a little nourishment any day now.

Housekeeping is disaster-fraught, you see, no matter how

long you've been at it. For this reason, it is important to know the following deep-breathing exercise to help calm you down in a crisis:

> Lie on your back, if possible, with your hands down at your sides.

> Shut your mouth, and keep it shut, as you breathe deeply as you can from way down in your stomach, letting the air finally puff out your cheeks.

> Let it out, *very* slowly with your cheeks still puffed, until your stomach is as flat as your own personal stomach was ever meant to be.

My friend would have recovered from her experience faster, I am sure, had she lain right down and done this, and I know the symphony conductor would have understood.

Z is for Zippers

You aren't so apt to have trouble with them if you make sure they're zipped shut when you throw the clothes into the washer.

3: Stains, Spots, Blots, Scars, and Dueling Wounds

*"Embarrassment may be avoided if you use pastry
brushes with black bristles. Then, should
they come out, you will be able to find them
easily and can remove them at once."*

—SOME HOUSEHOLD BOOK OR OTHER

I HAVE BEEN embarrassed by many things in my life, but
never by my pastry-brush bristles. This is true of most
women, I believe. Of all the things one has to blush over
in this world, the color of one's pastry-brush bristles comes
at the absolute tail end of the list.

But this approach is characteristic of most home experts.
They truly want to be helpful, but they go too far; and in
doing so, they set up too many straw men to knock over.

In this chapter I hope to deal with no straw men, just some Stains and a few minuscule Home Repairs. Inasmuch as we'll touch only on those that the random or reluctant housekeeper can see herself tackling, it shouldn't be a very long chapter.

All about Stains

Much unnecessary to-do has been made about stains. Any prospective bride who happened to read the Stain Removal section in a household-arts book would probably call off the ceremony, considering the whole business too sloppy to embark on, as well as too hard.

According to the manuals, she must know about oxalic acid and forty other queer things. She must maintain a Stain Removal Shelf too, in order to hold her own against a true tidal surge of spilled salad dressing, Mercurochrome, and Scotch-on-the-rocks.

Luckily, though, you needn't believe everything you read. For one thing, nice people simply don't go around spilling as much as these books would have you think. Weeks—nay, months—will go by during which the random housekeeper doesn't even see a stain, let alone try to remove one.

Spots, certainly. But nearly every one of them comes out in the wash when you use a good stout detergent and some good old sal soda.* (And if it's a grease spot on upholstery, you just rub corn meal into it and vacuum it the next morning.)

Also, the professional stain-removal ladies always stress prompt action. Ascertain what the stain is, they say, then whisk the stained object out of there pronto, fetch your little chemistry set, and get going.

Well, in many instances this is hard to do. If you are having guests, you can hardly turn to the gentleman on your right and say, "Pardon me, Mr. Fulmeister, but was that a puddle of French dressing or thermidor sauce you just spilled?" Even if he told you, it would be impolite to start treating the stain right then. The perfect hostess would see to it that she spilled a similar puddle herself, in order to put her guest at ease.

---

* Some people call it washing soda. Whatever you call it, you buy it at the grocer's for about 15¢ a box.

What is needed is a more realistic approach to stain removal.

I once asked an elderly nest-builder how to get a small, dark, oily spot of unknown origin out of my best damask tablecloth. She said to set the sugar bowl on it, in order to get another couple of days' mileage out of it for the family, and then send the cloth to the laundry.

I did, with truly excellent results. I found, too, that if two or three little spots were left over, I still had the salt shakers and the pepper mill left to work with. Most important of all, the years have taught me that place mats are better than tablecloths. Fine sheer linen ones are more than adequate for the not-too-dizzying circles in which I move. If one gets badly and mysteriously stained, which seldom happens, I can have it dry-cleaned for 25¢. If I feel like taking it to one of the do-it-yourself dry cleaneries, I can have it done for a lot less than that.

Here, then, are some general practical precepts.

Keep a heavy, long-handled candle snuffer handy for hitting people who forget to use it and who, instead, blow candle wax all over your table.

To get candle wax off your bare table top, you'll have to scrape it with a table knife, then get the rest off with lighter fluid. Or hot water, which I find works about as well. In either case, you'll have to rewax or repolish that part of your table top or buy more salt shakers.

To remove candle wax from fabric is even worse. You'll have to scrape it off first, then lay the material between two layers of white absorbent towels—paper or terry—or white blotters, and press it with a warm iron. Keep moving the paper around as it absorbs the wax.

Ideally this should do it. But, life being the way it is, it probably won't. You next fetch your can of cleaning fluid (there's a spray type you can get now which works pretty well) and give it the works, according to the directions on the can.

If the spot is still there and if the cloth wasn't much to begin with, you may now throw the cloth into the washer, with some detergent and sal soda. The spot will probably disappear eventually through a process of time and attrition.

If it's your best cloth, on the other hand, take it to the dry cleaner's.

In fact, any stained, expensive item you really like should go to the dry cleaner's.

You tell him what made the spot, if you know, then pray quietly. (Even dry cleaners aren't 100%, only 99%, as you'll find out if you ever get some indelible leg make-up on a white wool stole. Keep indelible leg make-up away from everything except legs.)

The place to start stain removal, actually, is at the department-store counter, before you buy something.

Even though you never intend to wash it, find out if you could. Later, then, if you feel overwhelmingly compelled to try to remove a spot, you'll know what you're up against. You'll know whether to try one of the washable fabric things, which we'll get around to in a minute, or whether to get out your trusty can of stain spray (mentioned earlier) which you use on nonwashable things.

And speaking of commercial preparations, you can buy good rust removers.

(If you ever want to try to remove rust the hard way, you can apply lemon juice and rinse with warm water. If the rust is in a porcelain sink or something, you can rub it with table salt and turpentine. But there's no reason for rust anyway if you hang your drip-dry clothes on wooden or plastic hangers, and see to it that your faucets don't drip.)

In this stain-removal business you keep bumping into these small magics—things people would *like* to believe, just as we'd all rather like to believe in haunted houses and water witching.

Like tomato juice for removing ink. Soak the inkstain in tomato juice for ten minutes. And you think, how interesting!

But it doesn't work. The tomato was finalized long ago, but they're still improving ink formulas, and today's modern indelible ink can beat any tomato to a fare-thee-well.

If the material is washable and the ink is still wet, you can soak it in cold water, then wash it in strong detergent with a little bleach added and see how far it gets you. If it's not washable, you can buy a bottle of ink eradicator and mess around with it, but ten gets you twenty it won't work 100%, and you'll wish you'd taken it to the dry cleaner's. There are just too many ink formulas around these days.

And if you ever spill ink on the rug, don't put milk on it, or cornstarch. If you can't rearrange your furniture prettily, call in the professionals.

Then there is the onion bit, for removing a mild scorch stain. Rub the scorched part on a cut raw onion, saith the prophet, then soak the stain several hours in cold water.

Not only do you feel silly while you're doing this, but it affects the scorch stain hardly at all and wastes an onion.

A little mild bleach will cure a little mild scorch in a jiffy. See later on.

All this is rather like Tom Sawyer's spunkwater cure for warts. There was plenty of spunkwater, presumably, around that little Missouri town, and there was also an ever-constant supply of warty little boys.

Now about play clothes. A small child's play clothes were never meant to be spot free, except for the first five minutes he has them on. If you insist that they stay spotless anyway, you'll damage his psyche, and he will probably grow up with a hand-washing compulsion.

However, the things little children slop on themselves are usually pretty simple—chocolate, mud, ice cream, jelly—and in spite of what the manuals say about glycerine and whatnot, your washing machine will usually get them out with the aid of the sal soda we've been talking about.

Not gum, though. You can remove it from something by freezing it with an ice cube, then crumbling the gum away— about as revolting an operation as you're ever apt to engage in. You'd better just ban the gum, as the children's dentist told you to in the first place.

Then there's mustard. Try to train your children to prefer hot dogs minus mustard, because mustard can make a pretty mean stain. You'll have to rub it with glycerine, which few people keep around the house, and then bleach it. (You could try rubbing it with lard before you bleached it, but you probably don't keep lard around the house either, and who's going to go buy a pound of it for one little old mustard spot?)

So look out for mustard.

In this business of getting stains out of washable items, a big thing to remember is this:

TRY COLD WATER FIRST.

Doing anything else would be a waste of ammunition, like shooting a polecat with an elephant gun. A huge majority of stains can be banished with cold water, if they're not too old and tired and comfortable right where they are.

What you do is this: you put an old towel under the stain, and you pat it and *pat* it and PAT it, with your cold wet sponge or rag. Also you keep moving the towel around so there's always some clean towel under the spot. Then let it dry by itself.

(Ironing it dry can make still another spot, and you never will get out to lunch.)

If you're certain the stain is coffee, tea, or fruit, you can use

HOT WATER.

You do this the way your grandma did, if she was any good at these things. You stretch the material taut—using an embroidery hoop or a rubber band around a bowl. Then, with a kettle of boiling water in your hand, you climb up onto a kitchen chair, yell at the kids to get out of the way, and aim the water at the spot. In addition to splashing everything in sight, this usually removes the spot because of the force and heat of the water.

Just don't use hot water on a stain you're not sure about, or it may cook it like egg on an egg beater.

If these things fail you, you've still an ace up your sleeve. This is your jug of Mild Household Chlorine-type Bleach, upon which you may lean heavily.

It will get those coffee, tea, and fruit stains out as nice as you please if you didn't feel like climbing up on the kitchen chair. It will also remove ink * blots from paper (dampen a cloth with it, and rub the blot gently). It will whiten your

---

* If you get some on your finger, spit on the head of a match, then rub the match on the spot and wash it with soap and water.

white nylon things, and it will, also, remove stains made by

scorch   Mercurochrome
mildew   lipstick

and many other things. Just follow the directions on the label.

If washable material happens to be colored, and you're scared to death, you can mix up a solution of this same mild bleach, according to directions, then snip off a tiny piece from an inside seam, and drop it in.

If it disappears, you may assume that you'd better try something else. You may go down to the library then, if you still care, and get a book on Stain Removal.

Perhaps one of their suggestions will work, although—when you think of how many stains there are, from asparagus juice to whale oil, and how many fabrics there are, from old-fashioned uneducated cotton to Silcratexalon—it is amazing that anything ever works at all.

And if it doesn't, of course, back to the old dry cleaner's.

One more thing, before we forge ahead.

You may, at some time, have both a rug you like and a puppy you like, which is a difficult combination. But should this situation develop, you'd better mix up

½ cup white vinegar
with
1½ cups lukewarm water

and keep it handy, somewhere it won't get too chilly, perhaps in the cracker drawer of your oven. Then, when Mother's Booful makes a puddle, as he inevitably will, you may blot it up with plenty of lukewarm water, then sponge it with the vinegar and water, using the same towel or blotter routine we mentioned a while back.

In spite of this, the rug's color may change, where the spot was, and you'll have to have it professionally spot-dyed. But you'll have that good feeling that comes from knowing you tried.

Now for a few modest Home Repairs.

Perhaps you've noticed that the crafty folk who write repair articles often end their suggestions with "in most cases this will work," or, "generally speaking, you'll find this helps." This gives them an out.

Then, when you've tried all sorts of queer things to re-

move a white mark from a dark table top, and you're standing there in pretty puzzlement because none of them worked,
you can't blame the author too much.

And really you shouldn't. They didn't know what sort of
finish your table top had to begin with. If you don't know
either—as many a girl doesn't—the plot thickens.

While we're on the subject, this matter of white heat or
liquid rings concerns the random housekeeper more than a
little. For one reason or another, she seems to be white-ring
prone. So we'd better go into it.

You can cover a white mark with vaseline, leave it on
overnight, and see what happens.

If nothing does, try cigarette ashes. Apply a small pile of
them, pour on a bit of olive oil or turpentine, and rub the
spot gently. This can't hurt, and it might very well help. I
know a lady who swears by it.

Next, if you have to, try camphorated oil, which is also
highly regarded by white-mark people. Not that it's necessarily a one-day operation, you understand. You rub for a
little while each day, when you feel up to it. And then, one
morning—one bright morning in mid-March, perhaps, when
the world is warming and the daffodil shoots are a tender
young green—

Well, if it's still there that day, you can get down to work.
First, wash off whatever polish or wax is on your table top,
using warm water and soap. Then make a paste of linseed
oil and powdered pumice, rub the white mark, and rewax
or repolish your table.

Now you may forget about it. You've done your part. It is
now up to the table, and as time goes by, it will probably
heal itself. If it doesn't, you must rise above it.

Now for dents, scars, and scratches.

Few people know and even fewer people care that dents in
furniture can be removed by steaming with a hot iron.

I read, somewhere, how this is done. First, you wipe the
dented place with turpentine, then cover the dent with several thicknesses of damp cheesecloth.

Next, place a metal bottle cap, metal side down, right over
the place where you think the dent is. (You can't see it
now, so you have to guess.)

Now press it with a hot iron. The steam will swell the
wood fibers you see, and the dent disappears.

You can do this without damaging the finish, the article said, and I am Susan B. Anthony. Any random housekeeper who tries it on her nice old walnut escritoire deserves just what she gets. This is the sort of thing that *never* works for those of us of the casual persuasion.

Anyway, there's nothing the matter with a few battle scars. Grace Hegger Lewis went even farther. Perhaps you read her account of the day she and her husband, Sinclair, finished furnishing their first apartment.

The first thing she did was go around and kick the new tables and chairs, whittle away a few good chunks with a jackknife, and sprinkle a little water on the new blue velvet sofa. She did this, she said, because it looked as though they were afraid of their furniture.

Keep this in mind. Never let your furniture get the upper hand.

If you should want to cover up a scratch anyway, it is nice to know that it's easy.

Rub it with a cut walnut meat.

Or rub it with a cut Brazil nut.

Or use one of your child's crayons, if he has one the approximate color.

You can swab it with iodine, if the wood is darkish.

Or shoe polish.

Another good thing about shoe polish: *white* shoe polish will hide scratches on white woodwork.

Of course there are some things in the field of Home Repairs which the random housewife usually learns, in spite of herself, as she goes along.

In the nail-pounding department, you may have discovered already that you pound your fingers less often, when starting a nail, if you insert it between the teeth of a comb. Then hold onto the comb instead of the nail.

You probably know, too, that it is unwise to drive a nail with a hammer into a plaster wall whammo, like that. Instead, you ever so gently dimple the wall with an ice pick, or some other pointed object, and then give the nail a gentle tap.

Also, when a hole in the wall becomes too large to hold a screw, many a girl knows enough to fill up the hole with something else. Wood putty, or—oddly enough—steel wool. *Then* screw in the screw.

And undoubtedly you know about epoxy, which sounds rather like a skin disease but is a perfectly marvelous sort of glue which holds anything together from grand pianos to wedded bliss.

It comes in two tubes—the glue and the hardener—and you mix it yourself, for whatever individual job you're doing: sticking towel rods on walls, legs back on chairs, handles back on cups, et cetera, et cetera.

But now let's back away from the trees for a moment—though we'll return to them presently—and take a look at the whole forest.

The first thing to know about Home Repairs of a more technical sort is a *good handy man*.

This may be your husband. Then again, it well may not. When it comes to fixing something around the house, many a modern husband is an inert mass. Perhaps this is because he doesn't *want* to fix things. It is equally possible that he doesn't know a faucet washer from his right foot.

Just because a man's a man doesn't mean he's a natural-born tinkerer. Many a boy grows up, in this specialized and urban age of ours, without ever having tinkered at all.

Don't force him, or you'll wish you hadn't. Forcing can lead to rough marital waters, not to mention the most sloppily installed traverse drapery rods you ever saw. Instead, look around for a man who is handy with his hands.

Perhaps it will turn out to be the community yardman, or the high-school boy across the street who flunks everything except Manual Training. Or perhaps there's an elderly widower down the block, who grew up in a simpler and cheaper time when you did it yourself or it didn't get done. Or advertise, with a six-word ad in the paper. You then save up your rattling doorknobs and flapping storm windows, and have your handy man come over periodically, for a nominal sum, and do them all at once.

The second thing for the random housekeeper to know is what is in her accident policies. It is a good idea to reread them occasionally.

The fact is, a number of Home Repairs probably wouldn't need to be made if it hadn't been for some fey maneuver of yours in the first place; and it is surprising what some of these policies cover.

I learned this myself, one social evening last winter, when we had barbecued the dinner on a small barbecue grill in the fireplace. After dinner I removed the hot grill in order to lay a fire, but started one on the hall linoleum instead because that is where I happened to set the grill down. It did the linoleum no good whatsoever, but the insurance people took care of it nicely.

And so, finally, to some wee Home Repair details and reminders.

Should you ever paint a room, or have a painter do so, save a peanut-butter jarful of the paint that was used. Ideally, you should stir this with a pencil periodically, to keep it ever at the ready, but you won't remember to. However, it will help anyway, because it is usually just the second day or so after a paint job is done that something ghastly happens to it which requires patching.

If you ever paint a ceiling, and if you wear glasses, you can smooth little patches of Saran wrap on the lenses, to prevent their becoming paint flecked. This would probably help when you're around things that steam up your glasses, too, like hot washtubs or Italian movies.

Your paintbrushes last longer if you drill holes in the handles to hang them up by.

Your paint can stays neater if you punch several holes in the gutter around the rim, so the paint runs back down into the can instead of outside it.

Your stepladder or worktable stays neater if you set the can on a paper plate. It will eventually stick to the can, which then has its own little saucer to lay a brush on.

REMEMBER: if you are only spasmodically artsy-craftsy, throw away that third of a pint can of puce paint when you're done with your current project. Otherwise these cans multiply like termites, and the paint all stiffens, and you could never use it again anyway.

If you *know* you'll use it again someday, pour some paraffin on top of the paint, and the paint won't have an inch-thick top skin when next you open the can. It will have a paraffin top though, and you'll have to operate as you would on a jelly glass. Some things there's just no clear-cut way out of.

As to wallpaper: you can usually flatten a bubble, if it isn't too big. Slit it with a sharp razor blade. Then, using a slender knife blade, insert as much thin wallpaper paste as you can, and press it firmly with a wet cloth.

Be sure you mop up the paste that oozes out. Wallpaper paste dries shiny.

If you must ever remove wallpaper from a wall, a paint roller soaked in hot water does a fair job of wetting the paper so you can peel it off. Try this before you tangle with the sort of wallpaper steamer you rent from paint stores.

But be sure you *have* to remove the paper in the first place. Often you can sand the seams and lumps, and if your new wallpaper pattern is a good busy one, it will hide the ones you missed.

You can usually unplug a vacuum-cleaner hose with a straightened-out wire coat hanger. Leave a quirk in the end to fish for whatever is plugging it up.

You can make a rug lie down and say Uncle, too. When a corner of it curls up, cut an L-shaped piece of heavy cardboard and glue it to the underside of the corner.

Also, if you have a slick little rug that skates around the floor, you can sew rubber jar rings to the back of it, and this will slow it down a bit.

Never forget the virtues of vaseline for curing squeaks, as in door hinges. It will also unstick things, such as the float-tank ball in that loveliest of television euphemisms, the Bathroom Bowl.

If you haven't any vaseline, you can still fix squeaks. Use talcum powder, or olive oil, corn oil, peanut oil, or any kind of oil you happen to find around.

A final word on Home Repairs. Someday a covered button may come off your tufted sofa. When this happens, you find a bobby pin and slip it through the under side of the button. Then, with the ends together, shove the bobby pin right into the sofa with the button bringing up the rear. The ends will open inside the sofa, and the button will stay on.

So much for that.

Now for Dueling Wounds.

Dueling wounds are of two kinds: those made by swords and those made by pistols. Somebody must have written a treatise on this sometime.

4: Don't Just Do Something, Sit There

". . . What, after all,
Is a halo? It's only one more thing to keep clean."

—CHRISTOPHER FRY

IT IS A FINE and heart-warming thought—if it be a random housekeeper who is doing the thinking—that there are numerous household chores you don't need to do. Many problems—if you don't face up to them—will go away, or will, in one fashion or another, solve themselves.

Very probably you've seen this work out in areas other than housekeeping. You may have noticed, for example, all the good time and energy wasted by conscientious people in trying to untangle their bank statements.

But one must remember, when the bank says one has six

cents less than one's figures prove, that one's figures don't prove anything. The bank is always right. Underneath your modern banker's pixie twinkle there lies mathematical genius. When he's not giving away lollipops or inventing Happy Time Savings Accounts, he's busily squaring the cube root of pi, just to keep his hand in. He could show you exactly where you misplaced that six cents so fast it would make your head swim. Remember, too, that there's not much you can buy with six cents today besides bubble gum. Sit easy.

Or let's say, as another case in point, that your car has developed a small plinkety-bleep under its hood. In the repair shop, the men in the white overalls can spend a good couple of days changing it to a plinkety-bloop. But if you had only sat tight and waited, it would probably have turned into a plinkety-bloop anyway, and a lot cheaper, too.

Now, the same curious forces are at work in the matter of housekeeping. Many things—regardless of what the experts say—don't need doing. This chapter concerns itself with them.

It goes without saying but I'll say it anyway that the true reluctant housekeeper needs a few major items of equipment (in addition to the fairly standard items more or less discussed on pages 93-95).

She needs, first of all, an automatic dishwasher.

One reason is that it hides a hundred sticky little secrets all day long and keeps your kitchen looking neater to the eye of the nosy neighbor. Secondly—and this is hardly news—it makes dishwashing and wiping unnecessary, thus saving you enormous amounts of time to invest in more interesting concerns.

Oddly enough, however, the random housekeeper is often hard to convince. She will say, "I can do dishes faster *my* way. People with dishwashers spend more time scraping and rinsing than I spend on the whole job."

Having spoken those exact words many times myself, before I acquired a dishwasher, I can explain this misconception. The reason you think this, if you do, is that *you have been watching Spotless Housekeepers at work.*

Spotless Housekeepers, you see, love to do things the hard way. Invariably, they get those dishes scraped and rinsed so clean that they need no further attention.

But they get it. Yes, indeedy, they get it. The Spotless Housekeeper then reverently proceeds to arrange those dishes in the dishwasher with painstaking and geometrical perfection. Only when this is finally done to her complete satisfaction, which may be two hours hence, does she turn the thing on.

This is wholly unnecessary. Get a dishwasher, then trust it. Trust the potent hot water too, and the good strong dishwashing detergent. Simply pick up the plates and scrape off any large object like a turkey carcass. Then, with a deft motion of the wrist, pass them swiftly under the hot-water faucet and get those dishes in there.

(If you have a small family and lots of dishes, you'll wash them only once every 24 hours, and food will have longer to harden on the plates. In this instance, it may make a certain frail sense to pass a wet long-handled brush over each object before putting it in the dishwasher. On the other hand, look at it this way: what if there *is* a tiny something left on a dish or two? You just wash *them* off, which is considerably better than washing off every single thing before putting it in, isn't it?)

The second badly needed major item is a self-defrosting refrigerator. Cleaning and defrosting the other kind is one of the household jobs most likely to get postponed from decade to decade. So get one. Buy it on the never-never, if you like, paying for it bit by bit out of the food money, but *get* one.

For purposes of clarity, this chapter has been neatly divided into three sections, the first of which is

THINGS YOU NEEDN'T DO AT ALL
and
THINGS YOU NEEDN'T DO HALF SO OFTEN
AS THE EXPERTS WOULD HAVE YOU BELIEVE

You really needn't scrub bathtub rings. You haven't any, you see, if you keep a plastic bottle of liquid detergent handy on the tub rim, and if you rigorously train people to pour in a capful, after they've closed the bathtub stopper and before they turn on the water.

I know a lady who moved into a new bathtub five years ago and has unvaryingly used this system—never scrubbing the tub—and it is absolutely as pure and white as the driven.

Most liquid detergents make foamy, thick, Cecil B. De Mille-type bubbles, too, which is an additional bonus. If your skin is allergic to detergent, some bath oils produce the same ring-free effect.

Also, you needn't iron pajamas or tea towels. Just fold them. Nor pillowcases, except for the guest room. If you live in a sunny climate and hang things outdoors, it's a shame to iron them anyway, for it lessens the fresh sun-and-wind smell.

(Incidentally, this gambit has a nice Thoreauesque feeling about it, as well as some snob value. It's kin to the upper middlebrow's unwashed salad bowl, and you can make conversational hay out of it. If you use a dryer, just smooth the pillowcases, fold them, and don't talk about it.)

And of course you needn't iron sheets. Use fitted ones for the bottom. If you haven't any, tie a knot in each corner of a plain sheet, tucking the knots well under the mattress. This does quite well at keeping a bottom sheet taut. Don't do anything about top sheets except to smooth and fold them, once they're washed and dried.

Don't iron your husband's handkerchiefs if he has a cold. Just fold them and, if possible, switch him to cleansing tissues. In fact, don't iron your husband's handkerchiefs anyway. Of course, if he likes to stick one nattily in his upper left suit pocket, you'll have to (or else paste them wet, boardinghouse style, on mirrors and windows, which is almost as much trouble and makes it dark in the bathroom).

But if he uses his handkerchiefs purely for practical purposes and keeps them wadded in his pants pocket, just fold them neatly after they're washed.

Now, admittedly this is a sticky wicket. Your husband and family are, after all, your own kettle of fish, and you know what they will or will not put up with.

But it is customary in most families for the husband to make the big decisions—like what to do about Red China— while you make the rest. And you might be surprised how unobservant many people are, just so something is clean and in the drawer where it belongs. You owe it to yourself to see what you can get by with.

Another useless operation is sorting bed linens.

The hell-bent housekeeper goes to a lot of unnecessary trouble sewing colored tapes on sheets, to differentiate twin sizes from full. But the thing to do, as you trudge through the years, is to either get rid of odd-size beds or acquire a wardrobe of sheets: all twin sizes striped, all full sizes plain, or something of the sort. Then you can stack them quickly, helter-skelter.

Also, I know a lady who lives in a perfectly lovely house and doesn't wax her kitchen linoleum. It isn't the kind the manufacturer tells you not to, either. She just sweeps it every day and damp-mops it once in a while.

She has found, she says, that water spatters make dull spots on wax and they show up more. As for the chances of the linoleum's wearing out sooner, she says she knows she'll be cordially sick of it in ten years anyway and will want another color, or else she'll have moved.

Although her system is heretical, we must remember that this lady has an equal chance of salvation with the rest of us; and she does some interesting things with her free time, too.

Another comforting thing to know is this: you don't have to polish furniture. If you'll give it a good coat of carnauba wax once a year, you just dust it occasionally thereafter, rubbing harder once in a while if there's a fingerprint. Next year, same time, wash off the old wax with soap and warm water and put fresh wax on.

Don't think you must clean out your fireplace after each time you use it, or every six times either. This looks bare and uninviting, as though you don't know what a fireplace is *for*. Also, a fire burns better if there is an adequate bed of ashes to hold the heat.

Then there's the oven floor. You won't have to clean it nearly so often if you keep a sheet of aluminum foil on it.

And don't waste time hunting for misplaced objects!

In most houses, things occasionally vanish into a mysterious fourth dimension. But they nearly always turn up, and they'll turn up sooner if you'll let them cool their heels.

The only time it makes sense to search is when it is something you need vitally that instant, like your car keys, and in this case you should have two anyhow.

Now consider, for a moment, canning and pickling and preserving.

Don't do these things unless you think they're great fun. Even though your neighbor is bragging about her seventy-eight pints of boysenberry jam, figure it out: unless the boysenberries, jam jars, paraffin, lids, and cooking power were all free, you'd have to keep right on canning for ten years to make even the tiniest return on your investment. You'd be surprised, too, how fast a family can get tired of boysenberry and want marmalade.

As for moths, don't do anything about them unless you're sure they're around. Otherwise you'll waste many a bright afternoon which would be better spent seeing your friends or practicing your judo.

Check with your neighbors, or the lady across the hall. If they've had problems, maybe you will. So then you can put your small woolen things into Mason jars with a few mothballs or a squirt of moth-fixer, and your bigger things, with ditto, into well-sealed plastic bags or cedar chests.

However, I've never done anything about moths in my life, except to cheer once when they kindly ate up a sweater I never liked in the first place. They haven't been back since.

(Some girls feel pretty smug because one afternoon they hung their woolens out to air, in the spring sunshine. But the moth eggsperts say that's a good way to assure yourself of a truly dandy crop of moths. The sunshine warms whatever moth eggs may be in the clothes, you see, and hastens the hatch. When the clothes get back into the dark closet, the moths will shortly bust out all over.)

And you shouldn't darn socks.

Rub the sock heels with paraffin or soap after every three or four washings, if your family is rough on socks.

But don't darn them, unless you're terribly broke and a marvelous darner. Otherwise, your family will have that touchingly poor-but-honest look. Also, the lumps may give them blisters, and you'll spend on Band-aids what you saved on socks. Unless you are willing to go the whole route, weaving back and forth through the material around the hole, so the darn won't fetch loose again next week, do not bother.

Don't mend rips in sheets, either, unless it is a very small rip in a reasonably new sheet. Then use press-on tape.

If it's an old sheet, it will tear again shortly in a new place. You might as well face facts and use it as an ironing board cover or cleaning rags. Or you could make some curtains out of it, some time when you're snowed in.

And for heaven's sake, don't scrub dirty cuffs and collars with a brush!

Don't scrub them at all. Wet them, then dip them in your bucket of soap or detergent beads so they resemble a little child's sandy feet at the seashore, then throw them into the washer.

Or soak them for fifteen minutes in a basin of hot water to which you've added a couple of tablespoonfuls of sal soda. *Then* throw them into the washer.

Furthermore, don't clean darkened aluminum pans you've cooked eggs in.

You can do it, mind you, by putting a quart of water in the pan and adding two teaspoons of cream of tartar, then boiling it for a while. But it will swiftly darken, next time you cook an egg. Just keep a pan for egg-cooking purposes discreetly in the cupboard.

Another thing: don't be too quick to call up and report a broken sewer line or the fact that the power went off.

Unless you live in an extremely lonely spot, this is foolish. The world is full of nervous Nellies who would rather report things out of order than eat. No matter how fast you make it to the phone, they will get there first.

I once knew a lady who, seeing her telephone pole go down in a brisk wind, called the phone company to report her phone out of order, and they said, "What number are you calling from, please?" and she said, "Why, mine," and then blushed herself into a rapid decline and has never been quite the same girl since.

Finally, don't wash spinach unless you have to. First, find out. Put a piece of cheesecloth, or a thin towel, in a colander, with the spinach on top. Run water through it. If the cloth stays sandless, the spinach is too.

As you can see by that last point concerning spinach, we are now scraping the bottom of the barrel. After all, how much of her lifetime does the average woman spend washing spinach? Precious little; and, whatever the amount, it serves her right for not buying frozen spinach in the first place.

So it is best that we press on to the second category, or

THINGS YOU CAN OFTEN NUDGE
YOUR FAMILY INTO DOING

". . . But in my heart, Truman will also go down in history for his attitude toward his undergarments—he washed his own."

                                              —LILLIAN ROGERS PARKS

Husbands needn't concern us too much here. Husbands, with few exceptions, do what they want to do and what they think they ought to do, in fairly equal amounts, and they are not easily changed.

Also they are illogical. Many a husband goes whooping off on a business trip, happily washing his own drip-dry shirts all the while he's gone, only to turn all helpless and fluttery at the sight of those same shirts when he gets back home, and *you* have to wash them.

Only you know what your own husband can be talked into doing. If you come, as I do, from a long line of Southern belles who feel that it is someone else's job to empty the wastebaskets, you may be able to get this fact across to him. Then again, you may not.

Or you may find, as I have found, that he likes to sharpen knives. This seems to bring out the warrior in some husbands. If you get him a nice little electric knife sharpener as a gift, someday, he may surprise you by keeping the kitchen cutlery in pretty fair shape.

If he doesn't, and if you don't know how to work the thing yourself, you can always take the butcher knife out in front of the house and give it a few swipes against the concrete curbing. This may frighten the neighbors, but it will put a fair edge on a blade.

Still, these are mere odds and ends. It is the children in the family who can help the most, because here you can call the shots. It will both strengthen their characters and sweeten your disposition if you do.

Children can do a great many things. Even though you have no cows to milk or wood to chop, there are still chores they can do in any Exurban, Suburban, or midtown dwelling.

At first it won't be easy. It will take a good week of standing with arms akimbo and voice raised, seeing that they do it and do it right. Many a mother has thrown in the towel on the third day, believing it easier to do it herself.

But this is shortsighted. Remember, in this world we drink a quart of vinegar for every pint of wine. Stay with it.

Look at the things a five- or six-year-old can do! He can:

1. Make his own bed every day. It will be a sloppy little nest at first, but it will improve with time.
2. Put his clothes back in the proper dresser drawers. You can explain clearly which drawer is for what. Then, when this goes in one head and out the other, as it very probably will, you can cut out magazine pictures of shirts, underpants, et cetera, and paste them on the appropriate drawer fronts.
3. Put his toys back in his toy chest, *every single one*.
4. Water the house plants.
5. Empty ashtrays.
6. Feed his puppy or his kitten or his goldfish.
7. Set the table.
8. Unset the table, *one thing at a time*.

Doing these chores can be the reason he gets his nickel-a-week allowance, if you like that system. However, many children have done them just because they jolly well had to, and they lived through it perfectly okay.

Then look at what a teen-ager can do, in addition to those things. He can:

1. Empty the wastebaskets, if your husband didn't.
2. Vacuum the car inside.
3. Wash the car.
4. Polish brass and copper.
5. Lay fires.
6. Vacuum rugs and floors.
7. Sweep and de-spot the kitchen floor.
8. Shine the silver. If you have him use silver cream, give him a pipe cleaner for getting in between the tines of the forks.

And if it is a girl teen-ager, she can do any or all those

things, in addition to ironing her own clothes, and your napkins and guest towels.

Of course, you needn't have a teen-ager in the family to get all this service, if you are willing to pay a modest sum for it. Indeed, most children work better for other mamas than their own. And most teen-agers need money for nylons and movies. I even know one who is saving up for college. This kind, especially, is usually happy to put in a few hours, one or two afternoons a week, doing the odd jobs you don't want to do.

To find one, just ask around, or go pin a note on the nearest high-school bulletin board.

And so we arrive at the third and final category:

THINGS YOU CAN PAY SOMEBODY TO DO

There is hardly a household chore you can't pay to have done, if it bugs you that badly.

Of course, paying for it hurts. It is one of life's little ironies that the lady who really needs professional help is the one who least enjoys spending money for it. Contrariwise, the spotless housekeeper usually welcomes assistance, so that she can clean her basement twice a day instead of only once.

But if there's a household job you particularly and truly loathe, don't believe the sunshine sisters who tell you you'll learn to love it if you do it *their* way.

I've read articles, for instance, on how to make ironing fun. You save it all up for the afternoon, they say, and you put on a Fresh House Dress. Then you open a window to catch the cool breeze, and you tune in the radio to your favorite program, and you sit on a stool behind your ironing board, and then you iron, pausing once in a while to crow with delight as you see the freshly ironed duds pile up.

But this is a lot of clam juice. You are still ironing; and if ironing makes you come all over introspective, you'd just better send your washing to the laundry. You can charge it off to Mental Health.

In addition to laundries, of course, there are janitorial and house-cleaning companies. You'll find them in the yellow section of the phone book in any fair-size community.

If you are rich enough, you can have them come one or

two days a week and do EVERYTHING, on a contract basis. If you aren't, you can decide what is your worst bête noire and have them do only that. Woodwork. Cleaning the oven and shoveling out the garage. Washing windows.

Or, if you are broke but desperate, hire one man for one hour and tell him to do his darnedest.

An advantage of these gentlemen—they are usually gentlemen and reassuringly bonded, so you can stay either in the house or out of it while they're in it—is that they bring their own soap and mops and buckets. All you provide is water and the pay check.

And, of course, in almost any town you can get housekeepers by the day, to come weekly or biweekly or whatever you can afford. If you are extraordinarily lucky, you may get Mrs. Rosemary Hayes, but you can't get her on alternate Fridays because that is my day. She is a professional housekeeper of intelligence and charm who has been my rod and my staff for more years than I care to count up. She considers the house her responsibility, and she sees to it that no nook or cranny is overlooked for too long. To each according to its need, she feels, rotating things nicely; and thus, in spite of me, she keeps the show on the road.

TO SUM UP: if you put your mind to it, and play your cards right, there are a great many things you don't have to do. Things could be worse, much worse, and let us all remember that, and count our blessings.

"What's the panel discussion about?"
"The Ordeal of Modern Woman is the subject!"
"You mean those two cars, automatic dishwasher, beautiful house in the suburbs but Something's Missing? That ordeal?"

—PETER DE VRIES

5: Dinner Will Be Ready As Soon As I Decide What We're Having

ONE OF THE more widely circulated myths concerns the young married couple in crisis.

The husband unexpectedly brings the boss home to dinner, and the wife either rises or doesn't rise to the occasion. (In the how-to articles she usually rises, adding a little sherry to the canned soup. In the made-up stories, she usually doesn't do herself too proud, although you get the impression that she'll certainly do better next time.)

However, if the truth were known, this situation scarcely ever develops in real life—unless the household is well-staffed or the wife is a superb offhand cook, in either of which cases there is, *ipso facto*, no crisis anyway.

You see, it doesn't take the average man long to learn that he married a random housekeeper, if he did, and random housekeepers are quite often, by their very nature, random cooks. Any reasonably bright Organization Man would no sooner think of bringing the boss home to dinner, unannounced, than of capping his jokes. He knows that if he did so, he would probably be an Organization Man no longer, or, at any rate, not with the same organization.

In this chapter there are approximately seventeen recipes for entrees, none of which you'd ever feed to the boss. I stress this because false claims are so often made for recipes —not intentionally, but through misguided enthusiasm.

For instance, the recipe ladies think up a new way to prepare creamed sea gull, and do it. Then, when they've ladled it onto quaint old Meissen plates and taken a picture of it all—the dull blue velvet cloth piped with military braid and the candlelight glinting through goblets of a most adequate little Rhine wine—they get all mixed up and start thinking the dinner is better than it is. But in the words of old Dr. Johnson, it still isn't a meal you'd *ask* a man to.

Neither are those in this chapter. These recipes are for the family.

The reason they are in this book is because of one inescapable fact which every girl must sooner or later come to grips with: housekeeping and cooking are miserably intertwined.

When you cook, you inevitably create the need for further housekeeping, as the crumbs scatter themselves about the kitchen floor and the wee droplets of cooking fat deposit themselves in a gentle film on the kitchen ceiling, no matter *how* many fans and vents you have. And, as you housekeep, you can't escape that tiny, harping voice on your mind's far periphery: "What am I going to have for dinner?"

As time goes along, most women discover or develop at least one staunch, totally simple stand-by. This is for the housekeeping days when they can't bear the thought of cooking, or for the days—equally painful—when they themselves have eaten a huge and lovely lunch or tea and can't stand the idea of food.

For instance, I know a lady who depends absolutely on Creamed Shrimp, and it hasn't let her down yet.

She keeps canned cream sauce on hand, and cans of cooked deveined shrimp. If there's a green pepper or an onion in the house—she doesn't worry if there's not—she

chops and sautés them in a little butter. All this she adds
to the cream sauce heating in the top of the double boiler.
And you know what is cooking, at the same time, in the
bottom of the double boiler? Eggs.

Finally, when the eggs are hard-boiled, she peels and
chops and adds them, with however many shrimps she
wants, or has, to the cream sauce. She lets it all get hot now,
and ladles it out on toast.

Another fast and reasonably painless operation is this:
slice any sort of sausage—garlic, Polish, frankfurters, or
what-have-you—and fry the slices a minute in butter. Then
prepare a box of ready-mixed potatoes au gratin, as the directions tell you to, stir in the sausage slices, and bake as
the box says to.

Then I know another girl—she didn't want her name used
either—who puts a touching faith in kidney beans and bacon.
She chops a couple of big onions and opens a couple of
cans of kidney beans and mixes them together. She puts
this in a casserole dish, with bacon on top, and heats it at
350°, until the bacon is crisp.

Of course, these things are peculiar to each family; for
their magic depends on their being something the whole
family *eats*. If your family likes kidney beans in the ab-
stract but not on the menu, this one would not be for you.

It's up to each random housekeeper to discover or develop one that is right for her family, then lean on it.

That is what the simple folk *do*.

This section begins, as most of us did, with The Egg.

There are seven egg recipes here—for the reason that you
usually have some eggs on hand. Maybe you don't have
some of the other odds and ends, but the lady next door
probably does. (All random housewives are on good bor-
rowing terms with their next-door neighbors.)

Observe closely, and you'll see that all these eggs are,
in one fashion or another, scrambled. Each supposedly serves
four people. If you don't think it will, you can add another
egg and a little more of whatever gives that particular recipe
its enduring distinction: clams, hot dogs, et cetera. Whatever
else you may say about these recipes, they're *resilient*.

The first is a well-traveled old recipe from high in the
Swiss Alps.

EGGELWEISS
serves 4

(First, spread some buttered toast with deviled ham, to serve it on.)

2 tablespoons butter

6 eggs

½ cup cream

½ pound grated Swiss cheese

2 tablespoons sherry

salt and pepper

an additional 2 tablespoons butter

Melt the first two tablespoons of butter in a skillet over low heat. Beat the eggs with the cream and add them. (NOTE: *if you haven't any cream around, as often happens, whole milk is all right. I suppose you could use slightly thinned canned milk, too, though I never tried it.)*

Now add the cheese and stir it around. It should melt promptly. When it's all thick and nearly ready to serve, add the sherry and the extra two tablespoons of butter.

Serve it on the toast you already spread with the deviled ham.

Notice that additional two tablespoons of butter we added up there. True egg *aficionados* say that this makes *any* scrambled-egg dish taste better.

ADVENTUROUS EGGS
(The big thing here is that you can add what you feel like adding to the chipped beef and eggs. It needn't be sliced artichoke hearts. It could be sliced green or black olives, or walnuts, or even some garlic croutons—although, if it were garlic croutons, it would be a little repetitious to serve it on toast. There is no salt in this recipe because chipped beef is generally salty enough.)

6 eggs

a jar of chipped beef, whatever size you have

2 tablespoons butter

a can of artichoke hearts, sliced

Melt the butter in a skillet over medium heat, then frizzle the chipped beef in it for a few minutes. Beat up the eggs, pour them over the chipped beef, add the sliced artichoke hearts or whatever you're adding. (If you use the artichoke hearts, don't use the frozen kind, for you'd have to cook them as well as slice them.) Cook it all for a minute until it's reasonably firm, then serve on toast.

EGGS RODRIGO
serves 4

(Rodrigo is a native San Franciscan. He says: Never use milk or cream in the eggs, strictly water. He also stresses the importance of slow cooking in an iron skillet.)

6 eggs
⅓ pound bacon (he prefers the canned Danish type)
6 teaspoons water
⅓ teaspoon Worcestershire sauce
¼ teaspoon sugar
⅛ teaspoon dry mustard
salt
black pepper

Chop the bacon and fry it till nearly crisp. Then pour out the fat and replace it with a good chunk of butter. Let it sizzle around the bacon.

Beat the eggs frantically now with the water and the seasonings. When foamy, pour them over the bacon, cook slowly, and stir constantly. Serve it on toast, or English muffins, or biscuits, or plates.

MR. PANELLI'S EGGS
serves 4

(This can be a good stand-by if your family is pizza-prone or spaghetti-minded or otherwise Italy-oriented.)

3 tablespoons olive oil   ¼ cup cream or whole milk
1 garlic clove,* crushed   ⅓ cup grated Parmesan
6 eggs   salt

* If some people in your family like garlic and some don't, omit it from the recipe. Then rub a cut garlic clove on the hot serving plates of the garlic lovers before you put the food on. I know a good German cook who recommends this, though I've not had occasion to try it because everyone I know likes garlic.

3 green peppers, sliced   1 medium onion, chopped
a pinch of orégano

Heat the olive oil, and in it cook the garlic, green pepper, and onion. When the pepper is tender, add the eggs beaten with the cream, salt, and orégano. Cook them slowly and when the eggs are set, serve them with Parmesan on top.

This is good with French bread, of course, and a green salad.

And now for a touch of the temple bells.

INSCRUTABLE EAST EGGS
serves 4

8 slices bacon, chopped and fried
6 eggs
6 tablespoons sour cream
2 teaspoons curry powder
garnishes if you have any

Melt a chunk of butter in a skillet over low heat. Beat the eggs with the sour cream and curry powder, pour it in, and cook over low heat. The sour cream will make it seem lumpy at first, but this smooths out. Salt, pepper to taste.

Garnish it with the bacon, some chopped nuts and/or candied ginger. Serve it with rolls or biscuits on the side.

CLAMMOND EGGS

(*This is a good Friday-night supper or any sort of late weekend breakfast.*)

First, see to it that you have some toast and bacon around and ready to serve with it.

1 can minced clams, drained
6 eggs
2 tablespoons butter
3 tablespoons cream or milk

Beat up the eggs with the cream or milk, add the minced clams, pour into the melted butter in your skillet—which is over low heat. Cook and stir till it's reasonably firm, then serve with the aforementioned toast and the bacon.

And, finally, a good down-to-earth recipe which children have been known to eat.

HOT-DOG EGGS

6 eggs, lightly beaten	1 tablespoon paprika
4 franks, sliced	2 medium tomatoes, coarsely
4 tablespoons butter	chopped
1 onion, chopped	salt, pepper

First, melt the butter in a skillet over medium heat. Then add the onion, paprika, and sliced franks, and sauté for five minutes. Add the chopped tomato and cook ten minutes. Finally, add the eggs and stir gently until they're set.

You could serve this on hot-dog or hamburger buns, split and toasted, or, of course, on plain toast.

These seven egg recipes—besides being fast and easy—are also cheap.

Now for some good fast easy cheap bean recipes.

CRANBERRY BEANS

A good-sized can of New England-style baked beans
  (*say, a 1-pound 3-ounce can*)
¾ cupful cranberry jelly, coarsely chopped
  (*there are 6-ounce cans which hold exactly that*)
1 teaspoon dry mustard
½ medium onion, chopped

Mix all this together and put it in a casserole dish. Bake it from 45 minutes to 1 hour at 350°, uncovered.

BEANERINOS

You'll need a slice of French bread or plain bread per customer.

Toast the slices on one side only. On the other side spread, in this order:

  plain yellow hot-dog mustard
  chopped green onions
  a good big dollop of canned beans
    (*any kind—tomato-sauce style or New England; they can be hot from the double boiler if you like, but it's not necessary*)

a good chunk of cheese
   (*Cheddar, Swiss, or what-have-you*)
2 or 3 strips of uncooked bacon

Slide them under the broiler, four or five inches from the heating element or flame, until the bacon is done.

Next we come to a meal-in-one employing beans of a different kind.

HAMMOND BEANS

(*or, depending on how you look at it, Beenzen Ham. You want to have a bottle of grocery-store barbecue sauce on hand for this one. If you don't, simmer these things together for 15 minutes: ½ cup chili sauce, ⅓ cup water, 2 tablespoons vinegar, ½ teaspoon prepared mustard, ¼ teaspoon plain salt, onion salt, or garlic salt, ½ teaspoon sugar. But this takes—to repeat—15 minutes.*)
Also you need:
   a ham slice—whatever size and thickness will feed
                  the family
   1 or 2 packages frozen string beans
   1 can peach halves or pineapple slices
   brown sugar
   powdered ginger if you like it

First, cook the beans and drain them. Then put them in the broiler pan. Now slash the fat edges of the ham slice so they won't curl. Brush it on both sides with the barbecue sauce. Then lay it on the broiler rack (over the pan with the beans in it).

Broil one side. Then turn it, and, before you broil the other, arrange the peach halves or pineapple slices, sprinkled with brown sugar and ginger, on the sides so that they'll broil too.

The barbecue sauce and ham juice, plus a little fruit juice, drip into the beans as it all cooks, you see, and everything gets pleasantly intimate.

In this matter of reasonably instant suppers, remember hot, thick, filling soup. For instance, on a cold night:

BEANASTRONE
1 can bean-and-bacon soup, undiluted

1 can minestrone soup, undiluted
2 cups water
1½ tablespoons butter
1 small chopped onion
¼ teaspoon orégano
1 teaspoon Worcestershire sauce

Fry the onion about five minutes in the butter, using a big deep saucepan. Next, stir in the bean-and-bacon soup, and slowly add the water. Finally add the minestrone and let it all get hot.

And you might give a passing thought to

CHICAGO CHOWDER

Chop and fry about eight slices of bacon, then pour off all but about two tablespoons of the fat. In it, sauté a chopped medium onion. Then stir in a seven-ounce can of clams, a one-pound can of cream-style corn, the bacon, and enough milk to make it the consistency you like—say about a cup and a half. Don't boil it—heat it in the top of the double boiler.

With plenty of crackers and fresh, canned, or frozen fruit, either of those soups will keep people alive.

If your family is cheese-minded, they'll probably like this next one. It's a rabbit or a fondue, depending on what you do with it; and it's simple, though it can seem rather polite if you want it to, for a luncheon or Sunday supper. (In this case, substitute one-half cup white wine for one-half cup of the milk required, and serve it in bowls, with broken-up French bread and forks for dunking.)

SWISS CHAMELEON
for 8

In the top of the double boiler thaw two cans of frozen cream of shrimp soup and one cup of milk. Stir in a pound of grated Swiss cheese, and when it's all smooth and hot, serve it on toast, rice, or English muffins. If you have one, a small can of cooked shrimp is a nice addition.

Now we come to

BASIC CHICKEN

Chicken is among the fastest, easiest things to cook, if you don't insist on making trouble for yourself by frying or stewing or Hawaiian-ing it. It is cheap too. I don't know what the chicken farmers are eating these days, and I hate to think what the chickens are.

Take a cut-up fryer, or your favorite parts thereof.

Brush each piece, on both sides, with olive oil, and sprinkle each piece generously, on both sides, with garlic salt. (Or onion salt, or plain salt and pepper.) Add a good dash of paprika too, for a prettier color.

Lay them on the broiler rack, six inches beneath a hot broiler. Remember to lay a piece of aluminum foil beneath them.

Broil the pieces twelve minutes, then turn them over for twelve minutes more on the other side. That is all.

BASIC BEEF

(This takes a while to cook, so you must keep this fact in mind and set the minute-minder so you'll remember to put it in. But as you can see, it's as easy as opening a can.)

> 4- to 5-pound piece of beef brisket
> a cut garlic clove
> salt and pepper

Rub the beef with the garlic, then salt and pepper it. Put it in a pan, cover the pan, and place it in a 300° oven. Cook it four to five hours, it really doesn't matter.

This doesn't come out pot-roasted, for some reason, although it does create a lot of good juice. You carve it like a beef roast, and serve it with instant mashed potatoes if you like.

Finally, one more dish, which doesn't belong in this chapter unless you cooked it the day before.

However, it fills an occasional real need—for instance, when you have descending upon you a number of people who are more interested in drinking than eating, and really don't *care* what they eat, so long as it's filling. Or when numerous children of all ages will be dining with you. Or when you aim to seek sea shells at the seashore and bring a Covered Dish along with you, to heat up later. This, then, is the time to make an

UNINSPIRED CASSEROLE

(*This will serve 8 to 10, amazingly enough, on a pound of ground beef.*)

 1 pound ground beef
 2 chopped onions
 2 cups canned tomatoes
 4 cups cooked noodles
 1½ cups grated cheese
 6-ounce can mushrooms
 ½ cup chopped pimento or green pepper or both
 1 cup ripe or green olives, chopped
 salt and pepper

Cook the meat in a little fat, then add onions and pimento or green pepper. Add the tomatoes and simmer three minutes. Then add everything else and cook, covered, for thirty minutes. Then take the lid off and cook for twenty minutes more.

This is as good a pedestrian dish as I know of. As you can see, it contains no canned peas, which is a plus factor in itself, and it goes a long way.

And speaking of Pedestrian. We will end this chapter with just a few practical suggestions which might conceivably come in handy someday for the random housekeeper and/or cook.

I know a lady who became tired of nagging her children to eat breakfast. Being rather a velvet-hand type, she couldn't just put the classic juice, cereal, and boiled eggs on the table and say EAT it.

So, instead, she changed the breakfast menu to applesauce and oatmeal-raisin cookies and hard-boiled eggs. Now they eat like lambs, she says, and don't catch any more chicken pox than anyone else does. Also, the children can fix this for themselves while she reads her paper in peace.

A green salad isn't so apt to get soggy—even though you've had to fix it in advance, for some reason—if you put an inverted saucer in the bottom of the salad bowl. Then the oil and vinegar can't collect in a puddle at the bottom.

If you ever want to peel peaches ahead, you can immerse them in half milk, half hot water, and they won't discolor. Then you rinse off the cloudiness before you serve them. This is a bother, and it makes more sense just to peel the peaches as you need them, unless circumstances are unusual indeed.

Another thing about fruits: apples—like tomatoes—can be more easily peeled if they've been in boiling water for a minute. You should put oranges in a hot oven for a few minutes too, before you peel them. Then all the white fiber will come off easily, along with the rind.

A lady who has had considerable experience peeling onions tells me that she has tried many ways of keeping the tears back.

She held a wooden matchstick in her mouth, but she still cried.

She peeled them under water and cut herself.

Then someone told her if she'd hold the onion upside down—*i.e.*, with the root end *up*, and then peel it downward—there wouldn't be so much juice. She tried this and it didn't work either.

At last report, she was holding a piece of bread in her mouth whenever she peeled an onion, and it was working pretty well. However, I doubt if it worked as well as using the dried onion flakes out of a jar or a box, which you can certainly do whenever you need just the onion taste and not the texture.

Onion flakes also solve the problem of getting onion smell off your fingers—though this is no real problem, in this day of deodorant soap. A bar of it handy at the sink gets any odor off your hands—onion, garlic, fish, or anything else I can think of. Just wash your hands with it.

It doesn't require half so much muscle to break open a coconut if you put it in a 300° oven for twenty minutes before you tackle it. When it cools it will probably crack open by itself. If it doesn't, just tap it lightly with the hammer. (Be sure to put it in the sink first, so the coconut milk will have someplace to go.)

Then there is plain ordinary milk. It won't scorch so easily, and the pan will be much easier to wash, if you rinse the pan with cold water before you pour the milk into it.

You aren't so often stuck for dinner ideas if you customarily carry a small cookbook in your purse. Then, at the grocer's, you may lean against the meat counter and plan your menu. Finding that there's a good special of Ground Round, you can check your little cookbook for something to do with it.

This way you aren't so apt to end up at home with an idea and no ingredients to carry it out.

As for whipped cream, it will stay firm longer—so you can whip it considerably before the guests arrive—if you whip it with either honey or powdered sugar (not granulated).

And here, finally, is valuable information concerning corn on the cob.

You know the way it is with corn on the cob. It requires precise timing; and even though your timing is precise, the family's often isn't. Either the corn is cold when it gets to the table or it is overcooked. So, when you cook corn on the cob, do this:

Start it in cold water. Add no salt—but—for four ears of corn—add two tablespoons of vinegar and two tablespoons of sugar. Cook it as you ordinarily do, then, for six or seven minutes.

Just keep the water hot, then, and DON'T TAKE THE CORN OUT UNTIL SOMEONE'S READY TO EAT IT. It will remain at the right edible point for hours. Also—so long as you don't take the corn out of it, the water can get cold and be reheated, with no ill effects.

And now, until a little bit later on, let us ever so quietly close the kitchen door.

6: How to Be Tightfisted without Having It Show.

MINGY is a fine old Scottish word that rhymes with *stingy* but doesn't mean quite the same thing.

Once upon a time, it is said, a Scotsman promised his small daughter a shilling if she would help the family to economize by eating no dinner that evening.

She agreed, and he gave her the shilling, which she put under her pillow when she went to bed. Later that night, when she was sound asleep, her father quietly removed the shilling. Then he gave her no breakfast the following morning because she hadn't taken care of her money.

Now there is minginess with a hey nonny. Indeed, it goes an inch beyond the proper meaning of the term. Our canny Scot was just a wee bit crooked with his wee bit lassie, and this, of course, isn't recommended.

There are ways and ways of being mingy. For instance, you can outfumble your friends at parking meters, or sidle up your stairway carpet to save wear and tear in the middle, or you can pour cheap liquor out of a good bottle.

Clearly, these things save you money. But people are bound to find you out. They'll eventually notice that you never have any parking-meter nickels. And you may start sidling up your friends' stairways as well as your own, through force of habit, which will look odd. As for the liquor, they're bound to notice how the empties of Old Cutthroat pile up on the back porch, while the label on the King Charles Pride o' the Regiment Scotch becomes increasingly streaked and yellowed with age.

Most Penny Pinchers, as the Home Economics ladies like to call these suggestions, are pretty worthless. Either they involve saving some dreary bits of food to do something even drearier the next day, or else they have you hanging around the grocer's, at the hour when he is clipping the whiskers off the old vegetables, at which time you can pick up some Good Buys.

However, the following ideas, which I have gleaned from some of the finest, chintziest female brains I know, make a certain amount of sense. You'll never retire on them, goodness knows, but at least you can't lose. In this day and age that's something in itself.

If your dinner looks skimpier than you thought it was going to be, see if you can serve something *first,* as a separate course.

This is basic psychology with a sound physiological basis. Formerly it was the custom to serve Yorkshire pudding as a separate course, before the roast. People filled up on it, you see, and ate less beef, which then lasted for another day, or possibly two.

You can serve your salad first, with plenty of croutons in it.

And soup, of course. You can combine a can of tomato soup and a can of consommé and a cup of water, heat, and serve.

Consommé, by the way, is very handy to keep around. You can add a half a teaspoon of curry or powdered dill to a can of it, and to make it look really top-drawer, float some avocado chunks on it.

Or you can serve the hot green or yellow vegetable first. There is a certain European pizazz to this. And when you serve it this way, you're less apt to overcook it.

You can also serve things *under* things. When you broil a smallish steak, for instance, put slices of bread—French bread if you have it—in the drip pan under the broiler. Serve the bread under the steak, and you have a fair optical illusion of more steak.

Remember: cheaters sometimes prosper.

And speaking of bread: always buy it unsliced and slice it yourself, as thin as you can. (This saves on calories too.) If you always keep your bread frozen, slice it when you bring it home from the baker's and *then* freeze it.

Another thing: while fresh parsley will keep for a long time if you wet it and put it in a covered jar in the refrigerator, it keeps best in the freezer. Wrap small bouquets of it in aluminum foil and put it in there. You can't use the frozen kind for garnishing very well, though, so you might as well keep a jar of it too.

Whenever you make hamburgers, always mix a grated raw potato with the meat. This stretches things a bit, and makes the hamburger juicier too.

And never throw away the inedible breakfast cereal the children sandbagged you into getting for the cute cutouts on the box. You can always crush it a little more and use it for casserole toppings or makeweight in meat loaf or meatballs.

Also: bread seldom gets so stale it won't make good French toast. This is great for lunch or breakfast any time, and it is a prettier brown if you add a teaspoon of sugar to the raw egg and milk.

Speaking of old stale food, one of the few others you can do anything pleasant about is stale dried-up cheese. Shove it into your meat grinder with a couple of good-sized chunks of raw onion, and grind hard. The moisture in the onion turns this into a good spreadable spread for sandwiches or canapés.

No matter how you, personally, feel about margarine, keep a pound of it around. Its taste isn't too easily detectable through peanut butter or other strong-flavored sandwich spreads, nor in many recipes that call for all butter but have a marked personal flavor of their own, such as chocolate or spice. Purist cooks wouldn't do this, but that needn't concern *us*.

You can get as much as an extra half-cupful of flour if you'll cut the ends out of your paper flour sacks, open them up, and pour. You get more sugar, too, by doing the same thing with paper sugar sacks.

Also, it is a good miserly move to pour a little water into supposedly empty catsup or chili bottles, and slosh it about. You can baste things like meat loaf with this, or use it to eke out the catsup or chili from a new bottle.

Finally, there is a much-touted system of making light cream whip by adding the white of an egg. The way you do this is to whip each separately, then combine them.

If it's a pretty fair light cream, this will work reasonably well. But don't try it with half-and-half—the half cream and half homogenized milk that passes for coffee cream in many places. It will be merely frothy, and it will never do for your Irish Coffee.

And, when you get down to brass tacks, there's not much difference between the cost of a half-cupful of light cream plus an egg, and the cost of a half-cupful of whipping cream. So it's really not worth bothering about.

So much for Penny Pinchers.

Then there is the minginess that is happily confused with fashionable spareness. Any girl who puts her back into it can think of dozens of these in a jiffy. Bare windows (*we couldn't curtain off that marvelous view!*). The light of one fat candle to dine by (*Ronald does so enjoy his chiaroscuro!*). No dessert (*Dessert is so banal!*).

In truth, of course, curtains cost money, and so do enough candles to make the food visible; and dessert takes some doing as well as some ingredients.

The best kind of minginess is the sort that doesn't bother other people and doesn't show.

As an example—to get right down to where the work is—if you frequently replace somewhat-used cakes of facial soap with plump new ones, you can chop or shave the old ones into Mason jars. Then you can add some boiling water, and the resultant soap jelly will be good for washing dishes, or fine lingerie, or the car, or a little boy's mouth out. In fact, you can spike this with sal soda to give it more vigor, and use it for washing linoleum and woodwork.

Notice the bonus here! While you're being tightfisted, you're seeming freehanded, because your family and friends are usually using fat fresh cakes of soap.

Then there is the more ordinary type of nickel squeezing which brings you no side benefits of that sort. But still it conserves cash, and offends no one, and is nobody's business except your own.

Like this: you can cut up an old rubber glove—across and across the double thickness, including the fingers—thus producing all sorts and sizes of practical rubber bands, and who's to tell? The children might, at their Show-and-Tell sessions at school, but chances are good that they'll find more interesting items to contribute, such as the fact that Daddy never wears pajamas.

Consider the case for the dishrag.

This is the age of the plastic sponge, but a dishrag is cheaper.

For one thing, it usually costs less to begin with—and of course you can knit or crochet them for nothing out of odds and ends of twine. Also, because a dishrag looks spiritless right from the start, you expect nothing else from it, and you put up with it longer.

A sponge,* on the other hand, starts out with a certain plump exuberance and ends as a festered lily, which you demote to the basement. But then you have to buy another.

Therefore it is good mingy policy to use dishrags and hang them somewhere out of sight.

The reason for all the to-do about minginess here is this: the random or somewhat trapped housewife often hates to spend money on things to housekeep with. There are so many other, better ways to spend it.

---

* If you're bound and determined to use sponges anyway, put them through the wash occasionally with a good dose of bleach.

Here again she differs from the spotless or career house-wife. When a manufacturer comes out with an 89¢ spray can of Mattress Pad Freshener, the spotless housekeeper hails it with delight. Now she has another little duty to perform, conscientiously and well.

But the random housewife's lower lip starts trembling. Being a little unsure of herself anyway, she thinks *maybe she should buy a can of it, if that's what everybody's doing. Not that there's anything wrong with her mattress pads. After all, if you wash them and sun them every once in a while— Still, though you don't have to keep up with the Joneses, you shouldn't slide back with the Kallikaks—*

And yet, she just doesn't want to spend 89¢ in that fashion. That 89¢ is just a little more than 1/320th of a one-way trip from New York to London—and from there, about 1/318th of a lovely cruise from Southampton to Cape Town.

Or it is 1/20th of a good permanent wave.

Or 1/10th of two theater tickets.

Or 1/2 a pound of pretty fair chocolates.

Or—if she has bread instead of hyacinths on her mind— if she is putting somebody through medical school or nursery school—that 89¢ still looms.

Scratch the Mattress Pad Freshener.

Here, then, for the minimum housekeeper, is a minimum list of cleaners that save money, as well as shelf space. For there's no point in cluttering your quarters with five differ-ent cleaners for five different objects if just one will do the job.

(This list doesn't include those pantry items—salt, vinegar, baking soda, and so forth—which you keep around anyway to cook with. We'll come to these a little later on.)

THE ROCK-BOTTOM EIGHT

1. The big soap jar, mentioned earlier
2. Washing-machine detergent
3. Cleansing powder
4. Steel-wool soap pads
5. Household ammonia
6. Sal soda

7. Household bleach, or Javelle water
8. Paste wax

Plus dishwasher detergent, if you have a dishwasher

Plus borax, in a hard-water town

This list isn't entirely my own doing. I've checked it with some mighty tightfisted ladies, whose houses nonetheless look quite as good as anyone else's.

One of them considered the list not rock-bottom enough. "Ammonia for windows?" she said. "Flapdoodle. Good hot water and an old linen napkin, *that's* all you need." And she does have shiny windows, as well as well-developed biceps. I've always thought ammonia or vinegar made it easier.

Obviously, there are as many ways to house-clean as there are to cure a cold. Your own rock-bottom list might differ slightly or radically from this one, and if it does, don't call me, I'll call you.

Now let's dolly up for a closer look at them, one by one.

1. *The soap jar*

If you use it to wash linoleum, add a little ammonia.

To wash anything painted, add some sal soda instead (the ammonia might hurt the paint).

For anything delicate, like car finishes or china or underwear, it's fine as is. After all, it was mild facial soap to begin with, before you gentled it down some more with the water.

2. *Washing-machine detergent*

You can use this for everything up there except the car, and a whole lot more—diapers, floors, appliances, and other things.

Just read the label. Those talented Home Ec girls at the larger soap companies understand the basic chemical difference between a soap and a detergent, which is more than I do, and you don't need to either, if you follow their directions.

Pay special attention to the part that says to rinse thoroughly whatever will be next to someone's skin—clothes, blankets, diapers.

3. *Cleansing powder*

Most of them contain bleach now, and that's the kind to

get. If the colors of the can label look terrible in your kitchen, you can pour the cleansing powder into a big copper, glass, or plastic salt shaker. Or use an empty glass jar with a screw-on top (which you punch a few holes in).

Notice that word *few*. Cleansing powder lasts longer if you're sparing with the number of holes you sprinkle it out of. The true mingy housekeeper doesn't uncover or punch out more than a couple.

4. *Steel-wool soap pads*

These are an orchid on a true rock-bottom list.

Instead of steel-wool soap pads, you could use wadded-up brown paper for scrubbing pan bottoms. Not to mention powdered eggshells, and let's not. These are highly recommended in Aunt Lucy's Compendium of Home Helps Including Etiquette Tips for Young Ladies.

Or, to clean an oven, you could mix scouring powder and ammonia into a paste, and scrub it with a brush or a rag.

You could get along without them, you see; you just wouldn't live so long.

But whatever you do, never get carried away and throw prudence to the four winds and use a *whole soap pad at once*! Cut it in half. This sharpens the scissors and makes the pads go further.

You can even baby those pieces, if you care that much. You can dry them in a warmish oven, after they've been wet, or over the pilot light. Or wrap them tightly in aluminum foil, so they won't rust away. (Don't keep one in a cup of water, though, as misguided experts have recommended. It will become unbearably slimy.)

In any case, wear gloves. Even though you don't have a manicure to worry about, the soap pad will roughen your finger tips, which will eventually rip your nylons.

Or, you can grip that little piece with a spring-type clothes-pin.

5. *Household ammonia*

This gives your sudsy water more enthusiasm.

Be sure to add the ammonia to the water instead of the other way around, or it will be awfully fumy.

You use it to clean the oven. Sprinkle some over the charred grease at night, shut the oven door, and leave it. In the morning it will come clean with a damp rag or, at the most, a soap pad.

Then there are windows.

Actually, the best way to keep your windows clean is to stop smoking. But an easier way to have clean windows is to wash them with a mild ammonia-water solution, applied with a piece of something lintless, like linen, or a chamois. A chunk of an old velveteen skirt, by the way, is a good chamois substitute.

If you ever do windows inside and out, remember to use horizontal strokes on one side and verticals on the other. Then you know where the smudge is.

6. *Sal soda*

The mingy housekeeper keeps a box of it by the washing machine as well as under the sink, because a couple of tablespoonfuls get things cleaner and brighten colors.

It's good for charred pans, too, like the pan you scorch the peas in. Add a tablespoonful to a couple of inches of water and boil it for five minutes. And add it to warm water and detergent to wash anything painted.

Another thing: it takes the misery out of washing oven racks. Fill a washtub with hot water, add a good couple of tablespoons, and soak the racks about an hour. Then the baked-on grease will come off with reasonable ease.

And use it for washing walls. Add it to the detergent.

(Remember always to wash from the bottom *up*.* If you start at the top and work down, rivulets run into the dirty part, like tears down a small boy's dirty face. They're hard to scrub out, too.)

7. *Household Bleach, or Javelle water*

These are mainly for bleaching yellowed or mildewed things or removing stains (see pages 37-38). Or keeping an old, somewhat pock-marked porcelain sink white; put a layer of

---

* At least, that's what the professionals advise. But I know a lady who disagrees. She has washed many a wall in her time and she says, "But if you wash from the bottom up, then dirty water eventually runs into the clean part, which is worse." I take no sides on this. Do it the easiest way for you, and don't use too much water, and rinse as you go. If you end up with a slight streak or two, just remember that worse things have happened and the world still wags.

paper in the sink, soak it with bleach, and leave it for half an hour or so. If it's a *new* porcelain sink, don't do this—the cleansing powder with bleach in it is enough to keep it white, and it's not so rough.

This Javelle water is a bleach you keep bumping into in household books. But just try to find any. Three drugstores I asked thought it was a cologne, and my grocer gave me a blank stare.

However, to give this book an authoritative note, I felt I should mention it. Indeed, I even went further, and got the recipe for it out of a Canadian convent where the girls bleach their own bleachables. If you ever feel impelled to make Javelle water, this is how:

JAVELLE WATER
1 pound sal soda
1 quart boiling water
½ pound chloride of lime
2 quarts cold water

Put your sal soda into a big enamel or granite pan, and add the boiling water. Now mix the lime in the cold water, let it settle for about half an hour, then pour the clear liquid into the dissolved soda. Bottle it and keep it in a dark place.

As you can see, this is a pretty stout mixture. If you spilled any, I'll bet it would dissolve the kitchen floor. I wouldn't think of doing it myself, with commercial bleach so readily available in nice plastic jugs, and I'll take no responsibility if anyone else does. It is included here purely in the interests of scientific thoroughness.

So back to the boughten bottled bleach. This is good for disinfecting objects like breadboards or chopping blocks, or sickroom dishes, if someone has something dreadful. On this last point, I feel—with many a random housekeeper—that a family germ is a family germ, and if you're going to get it, you're going to get it.

Still, there may be things our family hasn't caught yet. At any rate, it's a good point to keep in mind.

8. *Paste wax*
For the furniture and floors. Carnauba paste wax is best, because it contains the most wax. It's also the hardest to put on. You can get a liquid paste wax that's easier.

Don't use it on asphalt tile or rubber tile or a sheet rubber floor, though, or you'll be a sorry girl. The solvents in it will eat up the rubber, soften the asphalt, and make the colors run, and you'll have a true mess underfoot.

If you have this sort of floor, you might stop and ask yourself: *Do I really have to wax it at all?* And if you decide that you can leave it unwaxed and still finally meet your Maker unafraid, then do so.

After all, the only kind of wax you can use on it is self-polishing wax—which has a water base and doesn't last long —and you'll have a new career on your hands just keeping wax on the parts that get the traffic. So why not just keep it swept, and damp-mop it once in a while, and otherwise leave it alone?

The mingy-minded, floor-minded housekeeper must keep this in mind: the big thing with floors isn't wax, it's *buffing.* A good coat of wax once or twice a year—after the floors have been washed and promptly dried—is all you need.

For buffing, use an electric buffer if you have one or can rent one, or an old wool sweater wrapped around a heavy weight. Or have the children slide about in their stocking feet, or invite your husband to join you in a genial cha-cha. All this keeps the floors in nice condition.

Speaking of stocking feet, it's wise to keep a few pairs of Japanese straw slippers handy by the door, for female guests wearing spike heels.

That's because of those thousands of pounds' pressure each heel exerts on the half-square-inch of floor it stands on. Vinyl snaps back pretty well, but cork, linoleum, wood, and carpet don't recover.

One tends to forget this in the interests of etiquette, but your spike-heeled guest would probably be glad of a chance to rest her feet anyway.

If your husband is a vice-president or a stock boy who can sneak desk blotters home under his coat, have him do so. Or buy some. Then put them inside the front and back doors on rainy days, to protect the floors and the rug.

Another thing: a scrub brush nailed upside down on the porch makes a good mud scraper.

You may have noticed that nothing's been said yet about

Furniture Polish. That is because the wax takes care of floor and furniture both.

Now, where furniture is concerned, some people say Wax and some people say Polish, and you won't get any fight out of me. You just can't use them alternately, that's all— waxing a table one week and polishing it the next—unless you remove the old wax first.

Polish has a higher shine usually, and wax has a mellower gleam that lasts longer. Both work fine on porcelain appliances, if you ever want to go that far. You just make up your mind.

If you're of the polish persuasion, you can make it yourself more cheaply than you can buy it. It won't look as fancy in the old cider jug as the commercial kind does in the spray can, but don't think you're not paying for that spray top.

UNCLE HYMIE'S FURNITURE POLISH

Buy a quart of boiled linseed oil and a pint of turpentine and mix them together.

In this way you have a quart and a half of good furniture polish for about $1.30. The same amount of the other kind costs you about $2.10. Right there you've made 80¢.

And don't forget about *fronts* as well as tops. It's the fronts of chests and desk drawers that get the most finger marks. *Fronts are on the eye level of people sitting down.*

7: Salt, Soda, Vinegar, Lemons, or Aunt Lucy Done Tole Me

"Who won't speak out in black and white
Deserves to lose his copyright."

—EDNA ST. VINCENT MILLAY

IT IS HARD to be honest. Habit keeps getting in the way. But if you start by being honest about small things, you can work up to being honest about the big ones. So let us be candid, here, about a few pantry items and what they're good for.

The fact is, few of them do as good a job, as neatly or quickly, as things you can buy.

In the first place, most of the salt-soda-vinegar-and-lemon suggestions you hear originally came from Aunt Lucy's Compendium (published in 1862, last revision 1898). They're like a toasting fork compared to the modern automatic pop-up toaster with a dial-it-yourself color range and four slots for bread.

Also, some of them probably come under the heading of Aunt Lucy's Wishful Thinking. A pinch of salt in the water keeps most cut flowers fresh longer, she says.

Well, maybe so. I've done it and it didn't seem to hurt the flowers any. But I didn't do it under test conditions and so I never knew how long the flowers would have stayed fresh anyway. If you'd divide your peonies in half, sometime, and add salt to one vaseful and an aspirin to the other (there's a vocal aspirin school too), you might find out.

(The cheapest way I know to make flowers last is to keep on cutting their stems. Even when you've just snipped them in the garden and brought them in, cut them again. Otherwise their little pores seal themselves faster than you'd believe, and they don't get the water they need. You do this every day or so, as long as it seems to pay off.)

Still, many of these pantry odds and ends have their value, especially for the mingy housekeeper intent on saving every possible cent for more interesting things.

You never have to spend money for brass or copper polish, for instance, if you mix equal parts of salt and flour into a stiffish paste with vinegar. Then smear it on the object, the way you'd frost a cake, let it dry, rinse it off, and wipe it. Or just rub it, rinse it, and wipe it. (This is closely related to the salt-sprinkled-on-a-cut-lemon system but it works better.)

Some people say, "Why polish copper at all? Just lacquer it when it's new." But other people prefer a certain midway point, rather than the new, raw, pink look. And even though you lacquered it at the midway point, it would eventually peel and discolor anyway and need removing. If this is a brass fireplace fender we're talking about, or anything else that gets hot, the finish becomes not only scrofulous-looking but baked on, and it's a two-fisted day's work to get it off.

Here, then, are some of Aunt Lucy's old gags. Most of them save you some pin money and in any case are good things to know about. How else would you get nut meats out whole besides soaking them overnight in salt water?

Things to Do with Salt

You can add a pinch to whipping cream to make it whip faster.

Or sprinkle it on grapefruit to make it taste better.

Or add a teaspoonful to the water you're boiling a cracked egg in, and the contents won't ooze out.

You can remove perspiration stains with it. Use a handful to a quart of water, and soak the stained item for an hour.

And you can set colors with it, in cotton. If you're doubtful about the dye, soak the fabric twenty minutes—a quart of water to a half-cupful of salt.

You can perk up a fire with it. Throw a handful on, and then you won't need to fetch more kindling and start all over again.

You can sprinkle plain salt or rock salt on icy steps, in cold weather, to melt the ice. Just be careful it doesn't land on the grass, or on any place where you'd like to have some, come spring.

If you're not too softhearted, you can dissolve garden slugs with salt, into sad little puddles. Sprinkle it on them. Here again, be sure the slug is on the pavement first.

Then come in and gargle with it—a teaspoon of salt and a teaspoon of baking soda per glass of warm water.

You can clean drains with it too. A big broom-and-mop woman tells me it clears drains of grease and bad smells if you pour a strong solution of hot water and salt down the sink drain every week or so; and I see no reason to doubt it.

Then There's Vinegar

If you can't get the soapy feel out of something you're washing, add vinegar to the rinse.

Boil a little in a pan with a seemingly built-in fish or cabbage smell, and the smell will go away.

Vinegar cleans out narrow-necked bottles too. Pour in a little, with hot water. If the bottle or vase is in bad shape, add some pebbles or rice and shake it.

You can keep poached eggs from separating if you add a teaspoonful of vinegar to the water.

Maybe you'll like it for washing windows too. Add some to the hot water. Then if your feet are tired, sit down and soak them in it—just vinegar and warm water. For no good reason I know of, it makes them feel better.

And Consider Baking Soda

It's truly a tremendous polish for chrome. Just rub it on dry, using a dry cloth. Then use it on a *damp* cloth to clean oven doors.

And Consider the Lemon

It's good for marble. Wrap half a lemon in a cloth, dip it in tepid water, then in borax, and rub the marble surface. If this doesn't work, I don't know what will except for an electric buffer. If you can borrow one, do so, and it will restore the luster.

You can use the lemon juice in water as a mouthwash. It leaves a fresh feel and taste.

Or use it as a substitute for cuticle remover. Whitens the nails too.

A few drops of lemon juice will shine your shoes if you're out of polish.

Rub it on gnat bites too, if you're ever gnat bitten, and they won't itch so much.

And if you've all the time in the world and plenty of sunshine, you can remove rust stains with it. Let your rust-stained linen or cotton bleach in the sun, after you've wet it with lemon juice. If you don't have all the time in the world, see page 35.

And if you want to win the mink-lined sink for minginess of purest ray serene, start saving up and drying your lemon and orange peels to use as kindling.

What to Do about Bacon Grease

Like old razor blades, this often poses a problem.

If you use bacon grease to cook with, you can keep it in an old drip-coffee maker, and the sieve part will strain it. (You can buy grease-savers with built-in sieves, but it's an uninspiring way to spend your money.)

If you don't cook with it and have a good disposer, you can pour it down, but make sure you flush it with lots of COLD water, or the grease will clog the pipes.

If you haven't a disposer, or think you might want to use the bacon fat sometime but you're not sure, you can gradually fill up an empty beer can or soup can. This you can hide in anything you consider attractive, like a British toffee tin with a hinged lid, or whatever will cover up the beer can with reasonable aplomb. Then, when the beer can is full of hardened fat and you're tired of it, you put *it* in the garbage, but not the outside container. Then you start over.

Then there is the Note Pad and the Pencil. These are valuable for other things than grocery lists.

My mother understood their theory and practice very well. Understandably reluctant to see a whole batch of cookies disappear before dinnertime, she'd often leave notes in the cookie jar. When my brother and I reached in, after school, we'd find the loving admonition KEEP YOUR BIG MITTS OFF, which lowered our sights to graham crackers.

Also you need *labels* and *magnets*.

With the labels, you differentiate maple syrup from deep-fry frying oil, should they both end up in identical Mason jars. Or you mark frozen foods or premade sandwiches * and so on.

With the magnets—which come on little cards at the hardware store—you do this:

- stick a couple on the bottom of your vacuum cleaner, so they'll catch pins and tacks before they get into the bag
- or glue one to the underside of a kitchen shelf; then stick a thumbtack into the eraser of a pencil, and attach the pencil, thus, to the magnet, where it will hang handy and visible but out of the way
- or glue one to the end of a long stick, if you hate to bend over, and use it to pick up stray needles and pins when you sew
- or sew one or two to aprons or potholders so they'll stick to the stove or the refrigerator
- or use one to hold a damp dish towel to the side of the stove so it will dry quickly
- or use one to hold a recipe card to some metal surface, out of the way of the spatter
- or use several to make a bulletin board out of your refrigerator door. Just strew them about, like scatter pins, to hold papers
- or glue one of the little creatures to a waterpipe outside your house, as a good secret place to keep an extra house key

---

* Sometimes it's a good idea to make a sandwich for yourself when you make lunchbox sandwiches. Knowing you'll be eating the same thing, you may turn in a better performance. Put the mayonnaise between two lettuce leaves in the middle of the sandwich, so it won't soak the bread while it waits.

Another important kitchen reminder:

Should anyone give you a quaint old hand-painted wall plaque which says

> *No matter where I feed my guests,*
> *They always like my kitchen best*

cross out the final S in *guests,* and change *they* to *he* and change *like* to *likes.* Or, better still, throw the whole thing away, inasmuch as this particular wall plaque is hard on a sensitive ear.

Another handy kitchen item is a big dropcloth, the kind painters use. Spread it out to keep the floor clean, whenever things start to look messy, as on rainy days or at Easter-egg-dyeing time.

You can make handy kitchen gadgets, too, and amaze your friends, depending on how easily your friends are amazed.

If you need a knife-holder, glue or screw wooden thread spools by their bottoms to the inside of a cupboard door, as close together as they'll go. The resultant slots between them hold the knife-blade but won't let the handles slip through. (If you felt like it, you could paint them to match the cupboard door.)

And you can make a string-holder. Bore a hole through a kitchen shelf. Then find a squat, empty peanut-butter jar and punch a hole through its screw-on lid. Center this hole over the hole you just bored, then nail the lid down. Now put a ball of string into the glass jar, lead the string gently through the hole in the lid *and* the hole in the shelf, then screw the jar, upside down, into the lid.

On second thought, why don't you just keep your ball of string in an old tea-pot, with the end of the string threaded through the spout. It's a lot simpler; it just won't amaze any-body.

Furthermore, you can make plates stand up, against the back wall of a cupboard, by using a hairpin and cellophane tape, in this wise:

Bend the ends of the hairpin up, and spraddle them some-what, so they look like the legs of someone lying down, toes up. Tape this down on the shelf—toes toward you—so they'll catch the rim of the plate.

Finally, a few kitchen oddments:

A good way to clean the blades of an electric beater is to run the beater for a moment with the blades in a bowl of sudsy detergent.

When you make lids for lidless casserole dishes out of aluminum foil, don't throw them away—you can wash them off and use them over and over.

Now. If your kitchen hasn't enough eating room for little children, a cookie sheet across an open kitchen drawer makes an emergency table.

If your kitchen is infested with deep cupboards you can't see or reach to the back of, you'd better phone a carpenter and have him equip them with pull-out shelves on ball-bearing or nylon glides.

And if you'll stamp heavily on your big empty cereal and cracker boxes before you put them in the wastebasket, it not only relieves tensions but it enables you to cram more boxes in.

Finally, before we proceed to greener pastures and somewhat larger issues, let's take a look at three things you can do about Paper.

You can beware of buying many disposable items, like paper towels. It's cheaper to use terrycloth hand towels in the kitchen. If you feel you MUST have a paper-towel rack, put it near the stove. Then the towels will be used for draining things instead of wiping hands, and they'll last longer.

If you wrap many lunch-basket sandwiches, you might as well save the waxed paper that comes in cracker boxes. It's usually heavier than the other kind.

When you're out of correspondence envelopes, or don't want to buy any, you can mail the paper you wrote on. Write only on one side, fold the paper in thirds, and seal the open edges with any sort of tape. Then you address and stamp the outside surface, and the Post Office will accept it for first-class mailing.

You can get by without stamps, too, for in-town mailings. Just reverse the positions of your friend's address and your own return address and omit the stamp.

Then the mailman will return your letter to your friend for postage. Next, a big paddy-wagon will drive up and take you away to the federal pokey, for defrauding the U.S. mails. Thus you've saved five cents, plus board and room for the next twenty years.

9: The Rest of the Pea-Patch

"From Wibbleton to Wobbleton is fifteen miles,
From Wobbleton to Wibbleton is fifteen miles,
From Wibbleton to Wobbleton,
From Wobbleton to Wibbleton,
From Wibbleton to Wobbleton is fifteen miles."

—MOTHER GOOSE

THIS LOOKS like a big chapter from here, for I think it will involve large issues like Electricity and Ashtrays, as well as a tour of some of the rooms to see if we left anything behind. Perhaps we had better just jump into the middle and swim out.

All about Electricity
Electricity is like flower-arranging. Either you have a feel-

ing for it or you don't. The main difference is that if you
make a major mistake with your flower-arranging, you'll just
have a mess on your hands, but with electricity you can end
up French fried.

Most random housewives, being aware of this, are mighty
cautious, and this is as it should be.

If you ever want to know how to shorten a lamp cord, say,
have somebody *show* you. Don't waste time studying those
evil diagrams with wires marked P and P-1, Q and Q-1, in
the repair-it-yourself booklets. All how-to experts—whether
their subject is wallpapering or knitting or sex—tend to
complicate it unnecessarily. Some things you can only learn
by doing.

Take the fuse box. Every random housewife should learn
where the fuse box is, and how to replace fuses when it is
necessary, or when she gets tired of the old ones.

Her husband can probably show her this. So can the man
next door or the mailman. Men are natural-born fuse
changers anyway.

For years I meant to find out where our fuse box was. But
in the nick of time, we had our electrical system changed to
a circuit-breaker setup. This is a magical box in the basement
on which, when something blows, you merely flip a switch.
They cost about $50, I think, plus installation charges, and
they're worth every penny of it.

Speaking of men, a helpful thing to know about electrical
repairs—and it's about time we came to one—is that a man
usually gets faster results than a woman does when calling a
repair firm. There is something about the deeper voice, I believe, that works better. Any man who is handy will do—the
milkman, if he stops in about the time the washer conks out,
or the middle-aged paper boy—just so he has a resonant
baritone.

Now, if a fuse blows and you don't know what did it, *and
if you possess two extra fuses,* you can trace the source of
the trouble by doing this: unplug everything on that particular circuit—which means everything that particular fuse con-
trols. You can find this out, if your fuse box isn't labeled
with circuit directions, by seeing where the lights will go on

and where they won't. Then, when the bad fuse is eventually replaced by a good fuse, plug everything back in, one by one. When she blows again, you'll know it was—say—the toaster, and you will seem more intelligent when you finally present your problem to an expert.

Also: if an appliance stops working when it shouldn't, you might as well plug it into another wall socket before you give up. (Queer things go wrong with wall sockets too.) If it is a large stolid appliance that quit—like a refrigerator—put an extension cord on it, if you have to, for testing purposes. A heavy-duty extension cord, such as the one on your vacuum cleaner (page 29), is best, but in a pinch, to test with, you can use the regular kind.

And don't put a frosted light bulb into a frosted fixture unless there isn't much to look at anyway.

A big thing for the random housewife to know about electricity is the cost of it. (See also The Kilowatt, page 24.)

It is depressing, though not surprising, to learn that the things which are the most fun cost the most money, for the most part: the hot bath, the pretty music, the frozen goodies, the air-conditioned breezes. But you can sit and watch the clock or sew on your sewing machine for a mere two kilowatt-hours a month. (As we mentioned earlier, just find out what a kilowatt-hour costs, where you live, to translate them into pennies.)

The following list gives you a rough idea of how many kilowatt-hours you spend for what.

Understand, it is full of whereases and on-the-other-hands, because communities differ and so do families. If yours contains two female teen-agers who customarily have three baths and a shampoo daily, your hot-water heater can chew up a neat 600 or 700 per month. In the banana belt, an air conditioner can use a lot more than 80. And so on.

In general, then, this is how your kilowatt-hours go:

	AVERAGE MONTHLY KILOWATT-HOUR USE
Air Conditioner (*window type*)	80
Bed Covering (*automatic*)	12
Clock	2

Coffee Maker (*automatic*)	8
Dishwasher	30
Disposer, Food Waste	2
Dryer	80
Food Freezer (*18 cubic foot*)	100
Iron	10
Ironer	14
Mixer	2
Radio-Phonograph	10
Range	100
Refrigerator (*one temperature*)	30
Refrigerator (*two temperature*)	60
Sewing Machine	2
Sun Lamp	4
Television	26
Toaster	4
Vacuum Cleaner	3
Washer, Automatic	5
Water Heater	350

This leads us, unluckily, to some electrical equipment itself. In a gingerly fashion, therefore, let us touch upon it.

Any piece of reasonably new equipment is further advanced than is the random housewife. Although its many gadgets and possibilities fill her with innocent delight when the man explains them in the store, she doesn't do anything about them when she gets it home. She is a little scared of the rotisserie in her new pink double oven, so she continues to buy her chickens ready-rotissed. Then she uses her big top oven to thaw the food in, and the bottom one to warm the plates.

Another thing: whenever she acquires a shiny new status symbol—let's say that same pink double oven—it comes complete with an illustrated booklet.

Not knowing the model number of her oven, she hunts through the booklet to find one that *looks* like it. Usually she finds something that looks like it but not exactly—the timer is on the left-hand side instead of the right, or the burners are different. So, as she reads the instructions, she is never entirely sure they're talking about hers, and her sense of mastery is incomplete from there on in.

Or else she DOES find her model, which is XL-57, and she reads all the directions, with a gathering sense of triumph, until she collides with the final parenthetical remark ("These instructions do not apply to Model XL-57"). It is thus that the manufacturers maintain their happy state of oneupmanship.

Therefore, don't bother filing these booklets. Just heave them into a box or a drawer. In the first place, you won't be doing anything exotic with your model. Also, most equipment is staunchly built these days, unless you do all your buying at Discount House Fire Sales, and it always holds together until the day after the warranty period is up. And you wouldn't remember what you filed it under anyway— whether you put the instructions for your new automatic ice-crusher under A for Automatic, or I for Ice, or W for Wee-Krushit, its unfortunate brand-name.

Freezers and Refrigerators

A good thing to do with your freezer is to keep your sneakers in it, on hot summer days. Wash the pair you're not wearing in the washer, dry them in the dryer, then freeze them in cellophane bags. When you finally put your fresh-frozen sneakers on, they'll keep your feet cool for a couple of hours, even in very hot weather.

(Bras, girdles, and underpants feel better too if you keep them refrigerated. Not frozen, though—they'd be too stiff.)

Also, if the members of your family have strongly individual tastes, or, to put it another way, are absolutely loathesome to feed, a freezer can simplify things.

For instance, if someone likes salt-risen bread or pumpernickel and the others won't touch it, you can keep several sorts of bread frozen, if there's room left around the clothes. Frozen bread thaws so fast it's no bother.* Just drop the frozen slices into the toaster and toast. Or, if you want to serve it untoasted and you're hysterically anxious to thaw it out, you may hold a hot steam iron over each piece.

Then, too, if you're still awash with Christmas cookies, come mid-January, you can stack them in waxed cardboard milk cartons, seal the tops, and freeze them. They'll probably taste better in March.

But don't ever feel too guilty because you haven't many goodies in your freezer or your refrigerator. Remember, when

* And it's one of the few things you can refreeze without hurting it.

you keep specialties around all the time, they cease to be special and become staples. And remember way back when little children thought an ice-cream cone was a treat?

And speaking of ice cream. If you buy the kind that actually contains cream, you'd better keep it on the bottom and as near as you can to the center of the freezer or freezer compartment. If it's the skimpy kind that's mainly air, water, and skim milk, you needn't be so particular, because this freezes more readily.

(Also, you might as well save the insulated bags ice cream comes in. Then, when you have something like an opened can of dogfood which you want to keep cold but not very, put the can in one of the bags before you put it in the refrigerator.)

If you live in a stormy neck of the woods, with the power going on and off like fireflies, you'd better keep your freezer good and full. Then, if the power goes off, the food will stay frozen for forty-eight hours, which gives even the most sluggish repair crew a chance to get moving. If your freezer is only half full, things will thaw in twenty-four hours.

I know a lady who knows a lot about freezing, and though you wouldn't think it to look at her, she uses her old nylons to freeze things in. That is, she wraps them first in the foil or plastic wrapping, then shoves them into the stocking. This makes the wrap snugger and squashes the air out, which, she says, is greatly to be desired. Then she sticks the label, if she thinks she won't remember what the item is, between the stocking and the wrapping, and she can still read it.

She also says that freezing is like having triplets; once is enough. Whether it's raw food or frozen leftovers, don't freeze it again, she says, which sounds logical. A refrozen leftover leftover is repellent to think about, let alone eat.

Now, a new refrigerator usually replaces an old one; and if you keep the old one around, without using it, be sure you take the door off. Ghastly things keep happening to little children who set up housekeeping in old refrigerators.

Also, if your refrigerator isn't level, the shelves will become sloppier than they need to, and the door won't work right. Many new refrigerators have leveling screws at the two front corners. It takes two strong people and some rough talk to tilt it and level the screws properly, but it can be done.

Don't believe the old myth, incidentally, about storing nail polish in your refrigerator to keep it from thickening. It doesn't. Just get a bottle of professional nail-polish thinner and spike your polish with it periodically.

Another thing: if you ever have to defrost a refrigerator, fill big pans with boiling hot water and set them in it, once you've turned off the current. But don't fill your ice-cube trays with boiling hot water, because it removes the manufacturers' wax finish, and then your ice cubes will stick worse than they do right now.

And a good place to keep a cut lemon is on the refrigerator shelf. It makes things smell fresher, and you can still use it now and again to give a squirt to your string beans.

Should you ever buy a new oven, don't be led down the garden path by the pretty pictures of turkeys and pies baking visibly, and get one with a glass door. Glass oven doors must be cleaned with immense regularity or they look terrible. (If you are already stuck with a glass door, a soap pad and baking soda work as well as anything.)

Also, should your stove have a deep-well cooker, and you're happy about it, you'd better keep an inch of water in it, so the bottom won't burn out if someone turns the wrong dial. If you're not happy about it, you can have it replaced with a surface burner. Call a stove man.

I called a stove man once, for that very purpose, and got some advice, gratis. He said more ladies should get in the habit of using their automatic oven attachment. Then they wouldn't leave the oven on, so often, all night. He also told me always to leave the oven door open, when the baking was done, and the baking element would last longer. So I can do no less than pass these tidbits along. *Noblesse oblige*.

Other Things

Don't feed lye or drain-cleaning chemicals to your food disposer.

Nor glass, nor china. And, of course, anything metal will emerge redesigned, if it emerges at all.

If you're not hitched to a sewer and, instead, have a septic tank, don't give your disposer any egg shells, bones, or coffee grounds either. They'll eventually fill up the tank because the bacteria stand helpless before them.* In any case, you'll have to have your septic tank cleaned oftener, if you have a food disposer, but it is certainly worth it.

No sensible girl expects to cash in a dream at full face value. When the dream is a dishwasher, it is important to realize that a few disadvantages come along with it.

For one thing, not so many confidences are confided. Many's the good feminine heart-to-heart talk that used to be held at the kitchen sink while the ladies did the dishes. There is something about suds, time, and tea towels which gets you right to the heart of the artichoke, conversationally speaking.

This doesn't happen when you have a dishwasher. I really don't know how mothers ever get acquainted with their daughters today in dishwasher families.

Also, your bridge club is apt to land on you more often, without feeling conscience-bound to help clean up afterward.

You'll probably chip and break more glasses too. And you'll probably need some more flatware and china if you're to use the thing intelligently—*i.e.*, turning it on only once a day.

But most women find that its little drawbacks are far outweighed by its virtues. See page 46.

Then there is the matter of the bathroom floor.

If you're tired of the look of it, you can buy a cotton shag rug slightly larger than the floor and cut the rug to fit, with the aid of a big paper pattern (possibly made of newspapers and cellophane tape). Then you'll have wall-to-wall carpeting.

This isn't a practical measure, just aesthetic. Like the bald-headed man who has less hair to comb but more face to wash, you'll have less floor to wipe and more rug to launder.

And while we're in the bathroom, we might as well come to grips with another problem, which is the loud noise sometimes made by air in the pipes. Often this is easier to put up with than to do something about, unless you carry a plumber's card.

* And pay no mind to the folk who tell you to drop a yeast cake down the drain once a month to prod the bacteria. It won't, because the yeast lies dormant in cold temperatures and dies when it's hot; so it's a waste of money.

It can be caused by many things: the type and condition of the washers, or a loose screw somewhere, or an accumulation of air in the water—which last is pretty hopeless.

If it is a ghastly loud Squawnkkk which makes the whole house bounce, you'd better call a plumber, because the vibration could jar something loose. If it's only a resonant Bren gun sort of a *rat-a-tat-tat*, you can sometimes quiet it by turning on another faucet somewhere. I don't know why this helps, but it often does. Even if it doesn't, it gives you something to do with your hands besides wring them.

Then there is the matter of mirrors. Here, the true career housewife often adds bluing to the water she washes them with, because the bluing presumably gives them extra sparkle. But the random housewife just washes mirrors the same old way she washes windows. And if her teen-age daughter's hair spray has turned the bathroom mirror nearly opaque, she hands her teen-age daughter a bottle of back-rub alcohol, and a rag, and tells her to get with it.

When you're taking a bath, a good thing to remember besides soap is that the bathroom won't steam up so much if you run the cold water first. *Then* bring it to the proper temperature with the hot.

After a hot shower, you can run the cold water full blast, for a minute or so, to clear away the steam.

As for bath towels and washcloths, you avoid the whole His-Hers bit by assigning one pattern to each member of the family and screaming like a banshee if someone uses yours. In highly successful cases, a Pavlov-type reaction has been achieved. I know a man who never sees brown-and-white stripes now without feeling a strong urge to wash up.

Now for the bedroom.

It is nice to know that, according to Dr. Marie Stopes, a married couple enjoys greater nocturnal bliss by sleeping in a south-north or north-south direction.

Also, should your feet get cold because the blanket is too short, you can eke it out by sewing a broad strip of flannelette to the bottom. That part won't show because it will be tucked under the mattress.

And on extremely cold nights and days, pull the window shades down. (This goes for the rest of the house too.) You

see, the dead air space between the shade and the windowpane helps reduce the heat loss.

So, finally, to a quick trot through the rest of the house.

The Useful Box

One of the few good reasons for living with a cigar
smoker is that you're apt to have some cigar boxes around.
(Don't put up for a minute with a man who buys his corona
coronas one at a time.)

The twofold reason for these cigar boxes * is that they
are superb coffins for dead mice, should this be an item in
your family; and also, properly filled with things other than
cigars, they save walking. Ideally, every room in the house
should contain a Useful Box, although even one per floor
will help a lot.

Equip each one with
- a pair of cheap scissors (if they were good ones,
  someone would take them elsewhere for other purposes)
- a roll of cellophane tape
- a pencil and a ballpoint pen
- a small note pad
- spools of white, black, and beige thread, each with a
  needle
- a nail file

You'll even find the Useful Box handy in the bathroom.
You can use the tape to cover medicine-bottle labels, so
they won't get smeary. And it is smart, sometimes, to put
an additional label on the back (using the note pad and the
cellophane tape). If the doctor didn't tell you what's in the
medicine, and if the label doesn't say either, it's cricket to
ask him, and then paste his answer on the bottle. Then you'll
know, for instance, how much penicillin you've already
taken aboard, should the point ever come up.

(My grandmother used to translate cryptic pharmaceutical
labels into her own language. "For when Ben swoll up so bad,"
you'd read on a jar of ointment. This was handy in case
Ben ever swoll up again.)

* Most tin or wooden boxes will do, but cigar boxes are a tidy
minimum size.

Or you can use your Useful Box for writing occasional notes in the bathroom. A friend of mine heard that an acquaintance of hers habitually peered into her friends' medicine cabinets when she found herself in their *poudre* rooms. Whether she was looking for *poudre* or what, no one knew. And so, one day before this acquaintance came to lunch, my friend put a note in the medicine cabinet:

> *"What is it that you're looking for?*
> *Just let me know, and I'll be glad to help you find it.*
> —RUTH JONES."

No one asked her for anything, but at least—as my friend said—she felt she'd done all that a helpful hostess could do.

All about Ashtrays

An ashtray should resemble an ashtray: middle-sized, and equipped with grooves or slots.

Never use the dainty china chicken-bone kind of dish, which extinguishes your cigarette the minute you let go.

Never use the huge foolish birdbath type either. When four or five people are busy using it, it soon has all the allure of the city dump, and you must empty all fourteen pounds of it quite as often as the little ones.

As for the *objet d'art* ashtray, any decent guest would sooner use his trouser cuff than stub out a cigarette in a pale porcelain upturned palm.

If you're dead-set anyway on using your prettiest pretties as ashtrays, it is a thoughtful move to keep a few ashes in them at all times for bait. Then people don't have to ask.

Speaking of ashes, a house smells better if you empty all your ashtrays into something airtight before you go to bed. You can take them all out to the kitchen and empty them into the garbage sack and wash the ashtrays, if you want to. *But that means you'll have to carry them all back.* It is better to stroll dreamily through the house, last thing at night, with a big empty coffee can (which has a tight-fitting lid) and a damp sponge.

Next day you can do something about the ashes if you want to, but you really don't have to. If takes a long time to fill up a two-pound coffee can.

Also, if people in your house have a tendency to empty

ashtrays into wastebaskets—a regrettable tendency, as any Fire Department will tell you—you can line the wastebaskets permanently with aluminum foil. This helps a bit to fireproof them, and if the basket is a loosely woven rattan affair, it keeps the ashes from sifting out.

Speaking of the smells of houses, as we just were, they've yet to invent a better room freshener than two open windows and a cross draft, unless you happen to live next door to the sauerkraut plant.

In that case, or if you're in trouble smell-wise and company-wise too because guests arrive just after you burn the scrambled eggs and it's too cool to open the windows, you can burn a tablespoon of ground coffee on a hot stove burner. Or you can pour a little ammonia into boiling water and leave it on the stove for a bit.

Then, next time you think of it, in a grocery store, you can get a can of odorless spray deodorant, which is a lot better than the Old Oriental Patchouli or Sweet Verbena.

A decorator once told me that every room needs a sore thumb, to prevent the room's being a too-pat example of the department-store decorator's art. This is a comforting thought, on occasion, to most random housewives.

One sore thumb among many which I have been faced with is a large white bulldog who likes to sleep on a Victorian rocker. However, this problem was easily solved by a small mousetrap. If you put one—sprung and ready to snap —on the piece of furniture your animals are fondest of, they'll love it no longer. The mousetrap doesn't permanently damage their psyches, you understand. It just gives them a healthy respect for that particular sofa or chair.

And now that animals have sneaked in here—as they will, the moment you open any door—it's just as well to admit that a little bluing in the shampoo water does wonders for a white poodle. Also, if you want to make a new kitten feel supremely at home, touch his paws with tuna juice.

But back to the decorator's art. Should you have a group of pictures hanging together, and nothing better to do with your time, you can wrap cellophane tape around the part of the wire that goes over the hook. Then they won't get out of kilter, and everyone who comes into the room will Oh and Ah over how straight your pictures hang.

This brings us, finally, to the fireplace, where we can thankfully deposit all the bits and pieces of paper these notes were written on. But after the flames simmer down, the fireplace may look a little blank.

Well, if you're out of firewood or if it's bright hot summer, you can line up some geraniums, in red clay pots.

Or in Italian pottery pots.

Or, if you're so rich you don't give a hang, in white French soufflé dishes of nicely graduated sizes.

Or any sort of flower—real flower, fake flower—in any sort of pot—cheap pot, fancy pot—that your little heart happens to desire. For whatever queer things you choose to have around you are nobody's business but your own, and let nobody tell you different.

> *Stand fast, for to a good port hast thou rowed.*
> *Let not thy hope and courage e'er grow less,*
> *For only some great lack or some excess,*
> *Or overhaste, can make our labor vain,*
> *Whereby our happy end we shall attain.*
>   —TROILUS AND CRESSIDA

9: How to Be Happy When You're Miserable

NOW, THERE happens an occasional day, like the day before you have a baby, when your strength is as the strength of ten, and you stand amazed at all the big unpleasant jobs you actually *did*.

Then there are other days which lose their momentum before they ever get any, and the only sort of job you are up to is a small one, like twirling your cowlick.

There's nothing the matter with an occasional day like this. Indeed, I know a woman who makes a point of giving herself one, every six weeks or so. She simply muffles the phone and goes to bed for twenty-four hours, taking her books and manicure equipment with her.

Because it is understood that the rest of the family may have the same privilege when they think they need it, they co-operate. They bring her a cup of soup and a piece of cake for dinner, and otherwise stay out of the way. And she has a tranquil, therapeutic time, preserving herself in the amber of solitude and recharging her batteries.

But sometimes you stumble over a day of doing nothing ——or a series of them—which you can ill afford. For if you continue to stand immobile among deeds undone and resolutions vain, you'll find that you can't even do the things you *want* to do, and presently you may lose your mind. Every girl owes it to herself to hang onto her mind as long as she can.

The reason for these occasional periods of standing and staring while the work piles up is usually malaise of the spirit. It can stem from any one of three or four thousand deep-seated causes which there isn't room to tackle here, much as I'd like to have a try.

Still, we might consider some random antidotes which random housewives have found helpful, before we get down to the actual business of how to make the fur fly.

How to Comfort Yourself

Life being the daily affair it is, full of jobs that are done only to be done all over again, the random housewife often feels a bit like Theophilus Thistle, the unsuccessful thistle-sifter who thrust three thousand thistles through the thick of his thumb. There is no end to the thistles, nor to the loose ends.

Worse still—if she be young or youngish—the random housewife is often prone to Torschlusspanik, or fear of being locked in the park at night, after the gates are closed.

With several children of assorted shapes and sizes hanging at her hemline, and few adults to talk to (little children, however beloved, are notoriously poor conversationalists), she tends to overestimate the big bright world going on around her, all gaiety, song and dance, and here-we-go-gathering-nuts-in-May. Life, as she is living it, tends to look shabby around the edges and even in the middle.

At these times you must realize—should you ever be troubled by this—that it isn't all that big and bright out there, nor is it roses, roses all the way; and that the people who are out in it are also getting their share of the universal thump (see page 19).

At these moments, too, you may take three slow deep breaths. Then you can reread Ecclesiastes 3, and realize that it's true as true that for everything there is a season, and a time for every purpose under heaven. And if the fulfillment of your own purposes seems to be flickering with increasing uncertainty, you can consider the fact that Ogilby, who translated Homer and Vergil, knew practically no Latin or Greek until he was past 50. And that Daumier didn't start painting until he was over 40. And that Grandma Moses began painting in her seventies.

I also know a woman who just learned to water-ski at the age of 61, and looks handsome in her bathing suit too. You see, there is world enough and time.

And you can bear this in mind: Sigmund Freud once said that he did his best work in a condition of moderate misery.

Oh, there are numerous things you can bear in mind!

Then there are some practical, inexpensive therapies. For example, you can write an especially cheerful letter to someone, accentuating the positive even though you have to invent some.

(You may feel a bit like a tenement child who—watching his mother plug the cracks in the windowpane against the blizzard—exclaimed happily, "Gee, Mama, what do *poor* folks do that haven't got any nice newspapers to stuff in their windows?" But Dutch comfort has its place. Even though it doesn't do much for you, it may cheer your correspondent.)

A friend of mine has another way. On the theory that she couldn't be more miserable anyway, she devotes a day to doing all the repellent jobs she should have done long ago: cleans the coat closets, waxes window sills, answers old cobwebbed letters, mends her husband's workshop overalls. This seems to clear her decks.

Another lady finds a certain small salvation in walking. Hiring a baby sitter for two hours, she hops a bus for a strange and different corner of her town and walks home.

Strange and *different* seem to be the operative words. You may take on a double-feature movie, if you customarily do good works. If you customarily don't, go read to the blind children. And if you often ponder the eccentricities of your husband, switch to the vagaries of the U.N. The ways of escape and inscape are fortunately as many and various as the people who hunt them up.

Consider this one: a woman I know has an insatiable curiosity about how the other half lives—both the richer half and the poorer half. So she finds out, and this, she says, improves her morale no end.

She knocks at any door—any house she wants to see the inside of—and she asks if Mrs. J. Robinson Higbee lives there. While the door answerer is saying No and trying to figure out just where in the neighborhood Mrs. J. Robinson Higbee might be, my friend has a good chance to examine the décor.

I know a wise old lady, too, who says that every woman needs six friends: one richer and one poorer, one prettier and one homelier, one more intelligent and one less so. She can then trim her social sails to her prevailing emotional breeze.

Of course, there are the expensive small therapies—the new record, the book, the professional manicure, or the fabulous new hat, if you like hats—which last is the stand-by of the cheer-up specialists.

But the fabulous new hat assumes, of course, that you have some excitement to wear it to. If you don't, having one can depress you. Often, it is better to get a brave new pair of whatever you wear around the house.

And speaking of expensive therapies, a friend of mine says that the time she is most depressed is when the budget is. At these times, the only thing that banishes that forlorn, penniless feeling is to go buy something expensive. Not only does she stop feeling sorry for herself then, but she has an additional incentive for scrimping herself out of the hole, which she then proceeds to do with a right good will.

How to Comfort Yourself When You Have Acted like a Jackass

Everyone does this occasionally, and you shouldn't feel too upset about it unless it happens quite often, such as three times a day, in which case you must simply get used to it. Remember, other people like you as well or better for

it, because it makes them feel so superior; so you've at least
spread a little sunshine. And at the *very* least, you've served
as a bad example.

And so—assuming that you're now in the proper frame
of mind to accomplish something—let's ponder:

How to Do a Lot of Things at Once

Let us say you feel it's important, for some reason, that tomorrow you make five dozen cookies for the Bluebirds,
wash and iron the bedroom curtains, write a long chatty
letter to the family, and shorten a skirt, which is a frolic-
some Monday for you, but there it *is*.

Now, here is where the efficiency experts say, Make a list!
Then, with a high-hearted feeling of accomplishment, you
cross off each job, one by one, as you get it done.

Of course, that's one way. But for the random housewife, it seldom works too well. Often you get such a feeling
of virtue from merely making the list that you don't feel
compelled to do any of the things on it.

No, you need a bigger burr under your bustle.

So. The night before, as you're going to sleep, you visualize the results you aim to achieve: the family letter written, the cookies made and packed, and so on.

Then, next morning you forget whatever your fourth-
grade teacher told you about finishing one job before
starting another, and *you start all four projects at once.*

You stamp and address an envelope and write a para-
graph or so of the letter.

You sift the dry ingredients for the cookies.

You slide the curtains off the rods, into a sullen heap on
the floor.

You set up the sewing machine and wind the right thread
onto the bobbin, and you set up the iron and the ironing
board.

And now you're royally stuck. You've brought yourself
to the point of no return. You'd feel a little foolish about
rehanging the curtains without washing them. You certainly
can't unsift the dry ingredients. You're definitely not about
to waste all that good bobbin work. And there is the desk,
with the letter well started, stamped, addressed—

You must forge ahead, that's all, and, often as not, you
do.

Housekeeping on the Half-Shell

I know a girl who swears by this, when her agenda consists mainly of housework. She finds that she enjoys greater freedom of action with her clothes off. Therefore, when the family is gone, and she plans on a thorough job of vacuuming and scrubbing, she bolts the doors and draws the blinds, then strips to the buff and gets to work.

This system, she says, is good for everything except washing windows; and it's especially nice in hot weather. Also, it doesn't dirty any clothes. All she needs to do later is take a shower.

Don't overlook the merits of the telephone—equipped with a twenty-five-foot cord and a shoulder rest—when you are knee-deep in janitorial jobs. Phone jacks are handy too, and not expensive. A couple of them, strategically placed, will greatly enlarge your field of operation. With all these things, you see, you can be social while you work.

And this will help, too, to make your time count during duty conversations with long-winded telephone artists. I know a girl whose elderly auntie expects an hour's good telephone visit with her every day. She has no idea that her niece is getting her ironing done, the dishes put away, and the casserole made, all the while they talk.

Another thing: the twenty-five-foot cord can help you *end* a telephone conversation.

You carry the telephone to the front door or the back door—whichever the cord reaches most handily. Then you open the door, reach out and punch the doorbell button, and say, "Oops, the doorbell rang!"—which is, of course, quite true, and your friend can probably hear the chime at his end of the line.

(I know a man whose system is simpler. He just says, "Sorry—have to go—my phone's ringing"—which, he finds, works equally well.)

And now to the matter of how to make yourself do various chores that you know you'll never really *feel* like doing.

One good way is to set the minute-minder * if you have

---

* The minute-minder is equally handy for reminding the children to put on their galoshes for school, or reminding their father to take his briefcase or his pickax.

one, or the alarm clock. You set it for a specific time, with a specific purpose in mind. *When it rings,* you tell yourself, *I shall vacuum the dog.* (This is excellent, by the way, for getting the loose hair into the vacuum cleaner before it gets onto the sofa, and most dogs enjoy it.)

It is a matter of self-starting, you see. While the perfect housekeeper has no trouble here—for she is organized, or, to put it another way, in a rut—the random housewife must employ whatever small devices she can lay her hands on.

For instance, I know one who has invented a variety of Russian roulette. On small slips of paper she has written specific orders to herself. *Scrub out the oven. Dust the books. Clean the bathroom medicine cabinet.* To make the thing more sporting, she has included some pleasanter directions too: *Curl up and read for an hour. Have a hot bath and a facial.*

These stay in an old coffee can until some day when she's feeling more random than usual. Then she pulls one out and does it.

You may find it helpful, too, to time some specific little bugbear, if you can remember to.

Take that medicine cabinet we just passed. Cleaning and straightening it looms large, to many housewives. It is a job to postpone until the sleeves are rolled up and the bathroom is redone.

But if you ever timed the operation, you'd probably find —as I just did—that it takes about twelve minutes. (I was going at a steady lope, you understand, and didn't take time out to experiment with the lipstick I found behind the aspirin bottle on the second shelf.)

Now, twelve minutes isn't much. Neither is a minute and twenty seconds, which, I learned, is the time it takes me to iron a pillowcase. (This involves never letting go of the iron in my right hand, shifting the pillowcase with my *left* hand, and panting a bit.)

So, by hanging mental time cards on various jobs, you can cut them down to size, and possibly get around to doing them a little more often.

Another way to use time is this: when you've a job that you KNOW is a big one—like cleaning the basement—do it in half-hour chunks.

Tell yourself you'll do a half-hour's worth today, no more. (And possibly a half-hour's worth tomorrow, but don't promise anything. One day is as much as you can safely speak for.)

Then set the alarm clock, telling yourself you'll quit when it rings. And maybe you will, for you can, with honor. And if you don't quit—if you figure that now you've started, you might as well finish—well and good. You've just fooled yourself into getting the thing done.

It's a curious fact that you are occasionally faced with a miserable desk job that makes even housework look good. Maybe you must organize a drive or a club program or address Christmas cards or write a chapter of a book or a dozen thank-you letters.

If you're not careful, you may find yourself baking a cake in self-defense—no matter how much you hate to cook—or cleaning dresser drawers, rationalizing busily all the while: the family needs more home-baked goodies; Cleanliness of the Home Comes First, et cetera.

The best way to lick this situation is to give yourself a really excellent manicure, then get out of your blue jeans and into a suit and high heels. This prevents you from side-tracking yourself into Home Ec.

It doesn't keep you from phoning a friend to have lunch and go see the new exhibit at the Town Gallery, since you are now dressed for it. But then, where random housewives are concerned, few things in this world are totally foolproof.

Then there is the business of making time when you think you haven't any.

This involves, for one thing, salvaging bits and pieces of it, with all sorts of wee maneuvers, and people have wasted a lot of time writing books about this. They don't amount to much. Most of them aren't things you'd really *do*.

Still, on the theory that every little bit counts, you can carry with you—whenever you go out—a handsome *big* bag, as models do. This contains not only your respectable shoes —to switch into when you get to where you're going—but your copy of whatever it is you aim to finish if it kills you, or your list of French verbs (see Mrs. Vandertamp in the next chapter). Thus, you can fully utilize those golden minutes waiting through Peewee's ballet lesson or sitting in the dentist's outer office.

If you're on wheels more often than you're afoot, you can use the glove compartment of the car in the same fashion. It is good to keep a small cookbook in there, too, so you can plan meals without too much standing and staring in the supermarket.

It is also helpful to stock your glove compartment with manicure tools. The best-manicured lady I know does it all in the stops and pauses while she chauffeurs.

Another good thing to remember is this:

Should you ever need to confer with someone, do it at her place, not yours. That way you can leave promptly. (At your house, your conferee might sit and sit and *sit,* and it is hard to think of a polite way of getting her out.)

Then, too, if you want to save yourself approximately fourteen minutes a year, you can do this:

When you receive a letter from a good friend, and—after reading it—are full of the bonhomie which such letters often promote, you can jot down on the back of the envelope all the things crowding your mind that instant which you want to tell her about. This way they won't get cold, and six weeks hence—when you answer the letter—you can write a better one faster.

But these are mere gimmicks.

The unfortunate cold fact remains: making time, in any considerable amounts, requires major surgery. You must cut out an hour's worth of something and insert an hour's worth of something else.

Often, the simplest thing to cut is sleep. Perhaps you're in the habit of sleeping seven hours a night, though you could get along quite well—as many people do—on six.*

If this is the case, you can get up an hour earlier. (This is usually easier than staying up an hour later, for some husbands get sulky about this; and you mustn't disturb the felicity of the home. But they seldom care how early you get up.) You'll find that you can whip through a great num-

---

* And if you can't, maybe you can make up for it with a nap at some more worthless time of day, like two in the afternoon.

ber of things in that one hour, for an early-morning hour is usually worth a couple later on.

Or you can stop reading the morning paper in the morning. Save it for lunch, or evening, and get going.

Or skip it completely. As somebody once said, keeping informed by means of the daily paper is like telling time by the second hand on the clock. Maybe you'd do better to read a monthly news review.

Or let the children walk somewhere, for a change. Two miles to school won't hurt them at all, and it will give them a Hardship to tell *their* children about.

Or let your hair grow. I know a girl who developed a large resentment over the time she was spending at the beauty shop every ten days, plus her evening sessions of putting it up. And so she let her hair grow, long and straight, and she enjoys the time she saves, as well as the rather new personality she grew along with it.

Most helpful of all, perhaps, you can become an eccentric, which is easy to do. And then you need make no excuses.

My great-grandmother employed this technique to great advantage, and I have always admired her for it. She was a vigorous old lady, rugged as a Kansas workhorse. She enjoyed her friends too, but she enjoyed, even more, the fit and feel of her own rocking chair.

And so, when she was urged to go visiting, she would say, with a pensive look and an ever so faint yet detectable note of reproof, "But you know, I *never* go out." No explanations, no whys, no wherefores. Just the simple fact. And so it gradually became understood that her friends came to see *her*—never vice versa.

Only think how well she would have handled herself today, in these times of rummage sales and volunteer committees and coffee-klatches and all the other assorted time-consuming evils we've fallen heir to!

And thus, by practicing all these little ruses, or some of them, you may well hoard unto yourself enough time to climb the Andes (one Ande at a time).

Or improve your figure, or your golf game.

Or practice the cello.

Or just sit upon the ground, perhaps, and tell sad stories of the death of kings.

10: How to Remember and How to Remember to Remember

"You can make worms forget something they've learned by soaking their tails in chemicals."

—RESEARCHERS AT THE UNIVERSITY OF ROCHESTER

IT IS HARD to understand why anyone bothers to do this to a worm. Worms probably haven't much to forget anyway, and they certainly have handicaps enough in this life as it is. Researchers seem to spend their days researching the wrong things. Far more to the point would be some thorough groundwork on how to get the random housewife to *remember*—to remember to get more light bulbs and call the man about the weatherstripping, as well as the fact that there are usually two ordinary measuring cupfuls in every pound.

Science has done little about this. Therefore, the random housewife's earnest, muscular mind—for it often seems that our minds are mainly muscle—must depend heavily on Mental Crutches.

For example, I know a lady whose personal world used to come all untied whenever Daylight Saving Time rolled around —or away—because she couldn't remember what to do with her clocks. In desperation, finally, she evolved this:

Spring forward, fall back.

Now when spring comes, bringing Daylight Saving Time with it, she sets the clocks *forward* (get it?) and in the fall, sets them *back.*

Of course, this means she must do a double-think—nearly *every* mental crutch involves a double-think instead of the single-think involved in simply remembering in the first place.

Still, it is a lot better than nothing.

Take the case of another friend of mine, who tends bar with a tablespoon. This is because her husband habitually misplaces the jigger glass. And on those occasions when she herself was doing the honors, she was never sure how much liquor to pour into a drink, until she carpentered for herself an interesting mental crutch, as follows:

2 T is 1 ounce;
4 T (which reads like 40) is the Dangerous Age,
or the Age of the 2-ounce Highball.

It is easy, even for her, to cut this in half when she wants to build a milder drink. So now she is nicely straightened out, and I pass her stratagem along in the hope that it will prove equally helpful to anyone else who ever loses her shot glass.

I also know a girl who—regarding cooking as an unhappily necessary evil—has never been able to concentrate long enough on herbs to remember what they are for. So she ties them to various foods, in various odd ways.

"Cherviled eggs," she'll mutter to herself. This sounds enough like *deviled eggs* so that it sticks in her mind, prodding her to add some chervil to her—you guessed it— egg dishes. And on her good days, it leads her gently on to remember chervil for other mild foods like chicken or veal or potato soup.

She also has a way of remembering the basic *bouquet garni*. Although she tries hard to avoid any recipe that calls for one, on some few occasions she can't. So she says to herself, "Time to see the Bailiff and the Parson, Marj." This gives her Thyme, Bayleaf, Parsley, and Sweet Marjoram to tie up in a small square of muslin and drop into the stew.

Of course, many people have, or are stuck with, a mental crutch or two, on which they lean when the going is rough. "I before E except after C" has saved many a business letter—which was correctly dated in the first place only because the stenographer probably remembered that September Hath Thirty Days.

On the other hand, maybe she didn't call to mind that dreary verse at all. Maybe she remembered the number of days in each month by tapping her knuckles. In this system, the mountains (or knuckles) are thirty-one-day months and the valleys between them are thirty-day months. If you start with January, on your first knuckle, you can't miss, with the exception of February, which always messes up everything anyway.

I believe, incidentally, that the Knuckle-tappers slightly outnumber the Thirty Days Hath September group. As it was explained to me by a friend who tried both before she settled irrevocably for Knuckles, you might start off on the wrong foot with the poem—for instance, "Thirty Days Hath *December*"—and you'd be in real trouble all year; but your knuckles never change.

This business of How to Remember seems to divide itself—as neatly as these things ever *do* divide themselves—into four categories:

1. How to remember to do something
2. How to remember a number of things when you have no props to work with
3. How to remember where you put something
4. How to remember the things that are left over, like who wrote "The Barcarole," and the presidents of the United States in their proper sequence

First, then, about doing things.

Now, the reason you forget to do something is, usually, that you don't want to do it.

You'd never say to someone, "Remind me to collect my Irish Sweepstakes winnings tomorrow." But the random housewife does say, "Remind me to defrost the refrigerator" (or pay a parking ticket or buy a new vacuum-cleaner filter) —all these being projects with which she is not passionately concerned.

Like giving someone a secret to keep for you, reminding someone to remind you seldom works. You've unloaded the responsibility onto someone who cares even less than you do if the thing gets done.

Hence, the Number One rule is this: don't ask anyone to remind you. Remembering is, unhappily, a do-it-yourself project. But perhaps one of the following homespun helps will help.

You can wear your left shoe on your right foot, and vice versa, until the *fait* is *accompli*. This will look funny and feel funnier, but it often works.

And there is the wedding-ring ploy. Wear it on your other hand. (If you haven't a wedding ring at the moment, do the same thing with your wrist watch: move it from the accustomed wrist to the other.)

I have a friend whose system is more picturesque.

She has imagined for herself a Dr. Seuss kind of household pet. He is a nine-footed Gleech, with ears like bathmats and a multicolored mink tail. When my friend must remember to do something, she pictures him doing it. He is at the telephone, for instance, calling the rug cleaner. Later, she says, when she calls her pet to mind, she sees him there, and—ideally—this reminds her that she, too, should be doing just that.

Or write a memo on the bathroom mirror, using the corner of a damp cake of soap. This is far better than the bulletin board, which is usually full of old cartoons. The mirror writing jumps out at you.

Also: if you have a light-colored Formica kitchen counter and a lipstick you don't like (or a red crayon), you can write truly blazing reminders to yourself, and later you can easily wash them off. After all, the man who laid my counter tops demonstrated their endurance by stubbing out cigarettes on them, and what's a little lipstick.

On the other hand, a friend of mine has found that a penciled note pinned to her bra is best for her. It crackles or it pricks her; either way, she remembers what she wasn't supposed to forget.

Then I know another lady who doesn't go to all this trouble. She simply uses her forefinger as an imaginary pencil and writes reminders to herself on her forehead. It remains visible, to her mind's eye, until she has done it, and for her this works beautifully. (She keeps thirty-three cats, too, all in one little house.)

Now for the second category: how to remember a number of things when you are without a lipstick or a pin or a damp cake of soap, when you're unable to switch shoes or set a minute-minder—when you're driving, for instance, or soul alone, in bed, in the dark.

This is where the memory experts prove the stuff they're made of. They have proved, beyond the shadow of a doubt, that you can remember fifty things if you will first memorize fifty key words or pictures to remember them with.

But to the random housewife, or crutch lady, this doesn't make sense. In the first place, she hardly knows fifty things worth remembering, and if she did, that's what pencils are for. *Four* things are her maximum; and four key words which work for most people—because they are easy to remember—are these:

1. flagpole
2. red bloomers
3. tricycle
4. pig

As you will perceive after a moment's close study, flagpole is singular, like 1. Bloomers, being bifurcated, are double, like 2. Tricycle, with its 3 wheels, is triple; and the usual pig has 4 legs.

Thus, when you must depend on your head alone to remember some assorted things—say, to call Dr. Mason for a dental appointment, to leave the back door unlocked for the delivery man, and to pick up anchovies and butter at the grocer's—you do it in this fashion:

First you run Dr. Mason up the flagpole. You clearly

visualize him going up, probably flailing his arms and complaining all the way. If you think hard enough about him for a moment, you'll find him still stuck up there when you haul out your key words* and look at Number 1—flagpole. You will remember, then, to call him up, and you'll undoubtedly find him none the worse for wear.

And so on down your list. You mentally put the red bloomers on the delivery man, if that helps you to remember him, or you hang a pair from the front doorknob. You see a cheerful anchovy riding a tricycle. And a well-greased pig wallowing in a trough of the best butter.

There you are, with all four things tidily remembered. You will find, too, that your four key words are obliging about cleaning themselves up. Once you've called the dentist or bought the anchovies, your key words are bare of association again, and ready to reuse.

How to Write on Your Stomach

By using a middle-sized pad of paper and a not-too-sharp lead pencil, you'll find it easy to make notes in bed, in the dark. This is for those times when you are too lazy to get out of bed, or when it's too cold to put your hands outside the blankets, or when turning a light on would awaken someone else.

Put your left thumb across the top of the pad. Write slowly and carefully, only a few words to the line and to the page, making sure your pencil point frequently bumps your thumb. This keeps the writing from going totally downhill.

It will be legible the next morning, though it will look like spirit writing. For people who get their best ideas in the middle of the night, this is a valuable technique. For people who only think they do, it can be an educational and chastening experience, when later they read what they've written.

How to Remember Where You Put Something

The only way is to make a mental note—when you are putting something somewhere—of what you're putting it next to. As you drop your car keys, say, into the zipper compart-

---

* You *have* to haul them out and check them, at fairly regular intervals, or they won't do a thing for you.

ment of your brown purse, you visualize vividly the brown grosgrain lining of that compartment.

This is a pure double-think. It is twice as much trouble, but it gives you twice the chance of finding your car keys, *if* you can remember where you put the brown purse.

Indeed, there are many queer ways of remembering many queer things.

Not all of them are infallible. I know a three-year-old girl named Susan who could invariably find middle C on the piano after her mother had pointed it out to her only once. Her mother was impressed, naturally enough, by her small daughter's musical aptitude. But one day, after the piano keys had been cleaned, Susie couldn't find middle C any more. Middle C had been where the egg was.

Or take

> *A pint's a pound*
> *The world around.*

Actually it isn't, in some cases. Instead of a pint, which is two cups, there are 4½ cups of sifted cake flour in a pound, and there are 3⅓ cups of confectioners' sugar in a pound. And how about cornflakes? A huge awkward box is only 8 ounces, and think how many cups it would take to hold them all.

Still, *a pint's a pound* has been a popular kitchen crutch for generations, and I, personally, couldn't get along without it.

Then there is

> *Cooking rice—*
> *Water's twice.*

Meaning, of course, that you cook one cup of raw rice in two cups of water. This is a handy rule-of-thumb—especially if you keep rice in a canister and are consequently without the directions on the box.

Or

> *One big T equals teaspoons 3*

One of my friends mutters this periodically, to keep herself reminded; for it has always seemed wrong to her that such should be the case. She feels that—logically—only two teaspoons belong to a tablespoon. I was about to remind her that there are three feet in every linear yard too. Then I decided that it might confuse her permanently into putting 36 teaspoons into every tablespoon, and I didn't mention it.

Related to the rhyming crutches are chants and litanies. These are handy too, as music students have known for years. I know a Dartmouth graduate who says he'll never again be able to hear the noble second theme of the second movement of Beethoven's Fifth Symphony without hearing, in his mind, the words:

> Uncle—John—has—come—home!
> Uncle—John—has—come—home!
> Uncle JOHNNNN! Uncle JOHNNNNN!

Similar to this, and more fact-filled, is

> Bar-ca-role from Tay-uls of Hoff-mann
> by-y-y Off-en-bach, boop boop.

Offenbach wouldn't have cared for the boop boop, probably, but you need something there for makeweight, as you'll see if you hum it over.

Closer to home, the musical approach is handy for remembering telephone numbers that trouble you. For five-digit numbers, as most of them are now, the tune of the nursery ABC song works nicely:

C A 3 3   1 9 4   Mis-sus John-son lives next door

(or whatever pertinent fact you can dig up about Mrs. Johnson and make it rhyme). Admittedly, one should be wary of twig bending in this fashion, but still it's an easy way to teach phone numbers to little children.

Then, of course, there are dozens of stratagems to help you remember odds and ends.

Like the *g* in stalagmite. Not that stalagmites crop up every day, but still, when they do, it's good to remember that *g* is for grow; and if you think of grow, you think of growing *up*, which is what stalagmites do. This leaves only stalactites to worry about, but since they're always stuck tight to the ceiling of whatever cave you're in, they are fairly simple.

Along the same lines, there is the fact that a principal should be a pal. I learned this in the third grade, gagging slightly at the time, but still I haven't forgotten it. It didn't straighten out the other principal principles involved, but you can't have everything.

And there is Mrs. Vandertamp, to whom every French student should be grateful. This is a good way to remember the verbs that are conjugated with the helping verb "to be":

> *m*onter
> *r*ester
> *s*ortir
> *v*enir
> *a*ller
> *n*aître
> *d*escendre
> *e*ntrer
> *r*ester *
> *t*omber
> *a*rriver
> *m*ourir
> *p*artir

(This system—similar to the Magic Sentence, which we'll come to in a moment—is one which many a random housewife uses to remember lists. I know one who belongs to a club that is well supplied with Aims. Each club-meeting day, the ladies must rise and repeat, in unison, "Friendship—Love—Aspiration—Pursuit of knowledge." My friend couldn't remember these in proper sequence until she noticed, one lucky day, that their initials spell Flap. Now she has no trouble with it at all.)

Now, if you're troubled by your hand signals when you are driving—or if the drivers behind you are—you can remember them like this. When your arm is

---

* I asked the girl who gave me this list why "rester" appears twice, and she explained that she hadn't the slightest idea.

Raised—you're signaling *R*ight
Level—you're signaling *L*eft
Sagging—you're signaling *S*top

This brings up the whole unpleasant business of Left and Right. Many crutch people cannot remember which is their right hand and which is their left.

One girl I know has partially solved this problem because she happened to notice that she has a small freckle on the back of her left hand. She's all right in the daytime, but when it is dark she has trouble. Her watch is no help to her, because she can't remember which arm she wears it on.

Another friend of mine was born left-handed, back in the days before people were afraid to do anything about it. Her parents and teachers insisted that she use her right hand, and so she, in trying to co-operate, would always look first for the little mole on the back of her left hand, and that wasn't the one. Crutch people, you'll note, are fortunate if they're born a bit spotty.

A man I know tells me he watches to see which hand goes automatically for his pencil or pen, and this solves the Left-Right situation for him.

Thus, as we have seen, the mental crutch field is alive with tricks, rhymes, stratagems, litanies, and Magic Sentences, but the greatest of these is the Magic Sentence.

The reason for this is that you can make them yourself, so easily, and that they can pin down nearly any list of things that needs pinning.

Take the simple declarative sentence, *"Shirley shouldn't eat fresh mushrooms."* This was developed by a bride I know, to line up the ingredients for baking in their proper order.

Her mother-in-law was forever giving her good cookie and cake recipes, but in casual fashion. "Two eggs and three cups of flour and a cup of sugar—" she'd say. But now, by repeating her Magic Sentence, my friend is alerted to combine the sugar and the shortening, *then* add the eggs, *then* the flour, *then* the milk or whatever moisture the recipe calls for.

Magic Sentences are valuable in remembering any list of objects. Students have found them helpful in remembering the Great Lakes: San Mateo Horses Eat Oats. Also the planets, in their order from the sun: Mary's Violet Eyes Make Jack Stay Up Nights Perhaps. (This sentence assumes that you know Mercury from Mars.)

Medical students, naturally, use a lot of them. Finding it difficult, for some reason, to keep in mind the proper order of the cranial nerves—olfactory, optic, oculomotor, trochlear, trigeminal, abducent, facial, auditory, glossopharyngeal, pneumogastric, spinal accessory, and hypoglossal—they remember, instead:

> *On old Olympus' torrid top*
> *A Finn and German picked some hops*

and if you quibble about the rhyme, you must remember that these are Med students, not Lit majors. (They also have a naughty little sentence organizing the complicated bones of the wrist, which your family doctor can probably tell you.)

Then there is a dreadful Magic Sentence which does, nevertheless, give you the Presidents of the United States in their proper order. While not precisely practical information for most people, still it impresses the children:

> *When a joke made me a joker, Van had to poke*
> *the fiery poker but let jokes go. Hastily*
> *galloping across country, Harry cleverly made*
> *ready to watch his cool horse run to eastern*
> *Kansas.**

But perhaps the most all-around practical use of the Magic Sentence concerns geography, and city street names. Many citizens have some odd ways of getting around.

Otherwise reverent Seattle residents remember that *Jesus Christ Built Seattle Under Protest*. This straightens them out on twelve parallel downtown streets—two beginning with J, two with C, and so on.

In Los Angeles, you can find your way around with "From *Main* you *Spring* to *Broadway* and climb the *Hill* to *Olive*; oh, won't it be *Grand* to *Hope* to pick a *Flower* at *Figueroa*."

In downtown St. Louis, going from north to south, you

---

* If you can't remember this sentence, just memorize the names of the Presidents in order, and this will instantly recall the sentence to your mind.

can *Wash St. Charles' Locusts* in *Olive* oil lest they *Pine* for the *Chestnuts* of the *Market*.

In my own little neighborhood, I frequently have occasion to remember that *C*harlie *M*utters *L*oudly *E*very *S*aturday *E*vening. Thus I have Clifton, Myrtle, Laurel, Elm, Spring, and Elizabeth exactly where I want them.

And these are but four magic geographical sentences out of countless hundreds, doubtless used in countless cities throughout the length and breadth of our great land.

Many people, of course, never need or use crutches.

I know one of them. It is my good fortune to have a friend with a really excellent memory. When she was ten years old, she was helping her mother run the telephone exchange in a town we'll call Minooka, Nebraska, which had a population of about 1,800 during beet-picking season.

My friend knew the town's 500 telephone numbers by heart—and she still does, which has its drawbacks. She often finds it depressing to have her consciousness snagged by the familiar number on a passing car license and be forced to remember, in spite of herself, that dreadful Snedeker family whose phone number it was, some twenty-five years ago, back in Minooka. She adds hastily that she doesn't think it really hurts to have so much rubbish in her mind, because she considers the mind to be capable of limitless expansion.

But we crutch people don't agree with her. We can't afford to. We believe, with Sherlock Holmes, that the mind is a room of fixed size and must therefore be carefully stocked, else you reach a point where you must drop out a fact for every fact you put in.

We crutch people are mighty, mighty cautious. We store few facts. We know that if we filled up our minds with useful information, we would have no room at all for our crutches, and where would we be then?

11: How to Look As Good As the Lord Intended

I. CLOTHES AND SO ON

"If only her petals curled up a little more, she'd be all right."

—THROUGH THE LOOKING-GLASS

NOW, YOU'RE LUCKY if you care a lot about your clothes and how you look in them, or if you don't care at all.

If you care a lot, you give the matter creative thought and regular, painstaking attention. You develop, gradually, a sixth sense which sometimes enables you to understand what the fashion experts are talking about. And you're never caught with your hemline down and your only good gloves in your other coat pocket.

It is equally advantageous not to care at all. If you feel this way, you can wear your leather motorcycling jacket with your Tyrolean dirndl, ankle socks, and medium-heel pumps, and feel perfectly happy about the whole thing. Areas of serenity are scarce enough anyway, and if this happens to be one of yours, enjoy, enjoy!

It is the in-between person who is in trouble, the lady who cares only moderately, most of the time, but hugely once in a while. But—not having done her homework, so to speak—she is never exactly prepared. It is for this troubled spirit that the following notes are included.

For a number of years I have been spasmodically in and out of the Fashion World, as it is correctly called, for it is indeed a rarefied world unto itself, with its own language, customs, confusions, and mythology.

In my somewhat nervous forays into it, I have never ceased to marvel at all these, nor at the curious naïveté-cum-shrewdness of the happy children who inhabit it. They believe the funniest things. Or, at any rate, they expect *you* to believe the funniest things.

Not long ago, for example, I read a fashion article which stated that the well-groomed woman cleans out and straightens her handbag at the end of every day, adding a bit of cotton dampened with cologne to keep it fresh-smelling.

Now this is patently ridiculous. The cologne bit is all right, if it appeals to you, although the little wads of damp cotton tend to gather tobacco crumbs and fuzz. But, as every woman knows, the contents of a handbag, like good whisky in a charred oak barrel, ripen and improve with age. Let decently alone, as it should be, a handbag becomes a true treasure-trove of forgotten riches—forgotten, but stored against the day you unexpectedly find yourself with nothing but time and your pocketbook on your hands, waiting at the airport, say, or quieting a little child in church.

In my own fair-sized field of acquaintance, which includes some fairly fancy females groomed to *here*, I've never known one to do anything so foolish as to clean out her handbag every day.

Indeed, the fashion people inhabit a never-never land. And yet, somehow, they keep it going! And with one pronunciamento and another, they manage to keep many women vaguely ill at ease much of the time about what they're doing and wearing. Their marvelous double talk even euchres these ladies into buying clothes that make them feel more ill at ease than ever, once they get them home.

Thus, the fashion experts keep the old economy rolling. (At least it was still rolling when I checked the paper this morning. These days you feel that you must look quick.)

For instance, they do this. They tell you this is the year of the Lean Leggy Look. To prove it, they show you a group of short-jacketed, short-skirted plaid suits on a group of malnourished models who would look lean and leggy wearing circus tents, for they are all six feet two, with not a hip in the lot.

So, hopefully, you try on a new plaid short-jacketed short-skirted suit. But even though you are reasonably content with your five feet five inches and your hundred and eighteen pounds, you find that the suit turns you not Lean-Leggy but Short-Squatty. The pockets have been masterfully placed to widen a girl where she least wants to be widened. Then the brief jacket spotlights your newly broadened base, and the waistline has been shrewdly manipulated to add a good three inches to your own.

And if you are of the short-squatty persuasion to begin with, the little plaid suit turns you into a baby tractor, and you move out of that fitting room low to the ground, your gears grinding.

You see, the fashion experts won't face simple facts. They won't admit that those starved models are the ONLY people who could conceivably look lean and leggy in those fat-making suits.

And they won't admit that some people can't look lean and leggy anyway, no matter what they put on, nor is there any reason they should. There is room in this world for all kinds and shapes of people, and everybody has charm or somebody.

Now, if you're short-legged, very short skirts won't make you look long-legged, just cold. Optical illusion can go only so far.

And if you have a 40-inch deck, the plaid will up you another size while the broken line afforded by the short jacket will probably enlarge your stomach. (Fashion experts say *midriff*, but it's still stomach.)

If you want to look taller and slimmer than you are, these are points to keep in mind:

Avoid plaids, checks, and splashy prints. Avoid, also, cluttered blouses, sloppy sweaters, two-tone styles, most tucks, and all gathers, pleats, and broken lines.

This leaves you with the Basic Black and other dark colors, in a simple next-to-nothing dress, preferably with a vertical stripe or line of buttons to carry the eye up and down instead of sideways. It may well make you feel like somebody's aunt too, and if it does, you should leave it alone. It is better to look round and happy than lean and miserable.

And you should wear simple, dark, high-heeled pumps, because they make your legs look longer and slimmer, and your feet smaller. But if red shoes cheer you, and illusion heels are more comfortable, you owe them to yourself.

Also, according to John Robert Powers, you should focus attention high, with a handsome hunk of jewelry on the shoulder. This shouldn't be hard to do. But, he says, you should carry a *small* bag and hold it above your waistline (for a large bag dangling *below* your waistline will widen your hips.) This might be very hard to do. Many a woman's handbag is a desk and dressing table combined, and a small purse just won't work.

You see, we continue to bump into a philosophic point: perhaps looking skinny isn't the be-all and end-all. Which brings us right up to the matter of whom you're dressing for—yourself or your audience. Fashion experts always assume you have an audience.

Well, you usually do, but often it's not an audience you care much about. Like the clerk at the hardware store when you rush down, in your clam-diggers, to buy another pint of paint-thinner.

Maybe you are a Round-bottomed Pants-Stretcher who—so far as aesthetics are concerned—shouldn't wear anything bifurcated. It's true that even the best-designed pants can't camouflage a lavishly designed lady. It's equally true that pants are the only thing to paint in. So paint in them. Fashion, and how you look, is not the primary consideration at all times.

(Also, you may have noticed that it is usually men who sound off on the subject of pants for women. But they think that shorts on themselves are perfectly all right. Indeed, they seem to consider their hairy knees a real treat.)

Then take the matter of feet.

Perhaps you have odd-looking ones, with long prehensile toes or something. You will look better, of course, if you keep them covered up, instead of wearing open-toed sandals or thongs.

But to many very admirable people, feeling comfortable is more important than looking charming—another fact that the fashion experts won't face up to. And if this is the case with you, then put on your sandals and let your toes jolly well wave in the breeze. It's still a free country.

It's simply a matter of knowing what you're doing, and why, and when to do it. Naturally, when you *are* dressing for an audience you care about, and want to look as attractive as possible, it's best to cover up your less attractive features. Good Queen Bess understood this full well, back in the sixteenth century, when she designed that big starched ruff of hers to cover up her unfortunately long scraggy neck.

Then again, the fashion experts periodically come up with graceful articles entitled something like *Be Timeless—Go Classic!* But until they define their terms more clearly, this is a lot of laughs. These days the eager fashion people seem to call anything a classic which doesn't have KISS ME, KIDDO in fluorescent paint down the front.

Now, a classic is, or should be, something that doesn't change; something that will look as good in 1982—assuming that you and it and the world hold together—as it does this minute.

But about the only items I can think of, offhand, that fit those specifications—the way styles are booted around now —are handkerchiefs, overalls, and deerstalkers' caps. While this might be an effective ensemble, it isn't one you could wear everywhere. And so far as your other things are concerned, the hemline is bound to do you in, and pretty promptly too; and if the hemline doesn't, the shoulders will.

Take the classic cashmere jacket I bought, not many seasons ago, and for a handsome price too, thinking I could wear it— as they say—forever.

I did wear it happily, for quite a while. Then one day, in town, I wondered who the football type walking along beside me was, and then found it was me, strolling along beside myself in the plate-glass window, looking like a fullback for the Los Angeles Rams. The shoulders were somewhat padded, you see, and though I removed the padding, they still rode high, for I seldom gain weight on the tops of my shoulders.

Speaking of the eternally nervous hemline, as we just were, a bit of good news has come to my attention. *Your mink coat should be an inch longer than current clothes are. And as the hemlines climb north, you can turn it up as much as 2½ inches without harm. Feel better now?*

However, this is the only cheering fact I know about hemlines, which—like heroin—are easy to take up but hard to drop.

You know how it is: you're left with a sharp crease, which turns into a shiny line; and you can't sew rickrack on everything.

You can sponge that shiny line with vinegar and warm water, but unless you're a lot better at it than I am, it won't get you far. So once those hemlines plummet, after a steady rise of several years, it's bye-bye little classic, as every woman knows.

Then, periodically, the fashion people will do a piece on The Ensemble, or The Costume.

You get this all at once, if you can afford to, or else you add one Superb Piece each season (spending a large wad on each Superb Piece). But even though you do this, it seldom remains a costume very long—another fact the experts won't face.

The average woman goes through a season much the way a little child goes through a day, and you know how that is.

In the morning, you dress Peewee in his crisp navy blue shorts and his cute white middy blouse with the red-and-blue starred collar, and white socks, and red tennis shoes. A real ensemble.

By 11 A.M. he's spilled grape juice all over his shirt, so you remove it, substituting a plain pale-blue T shirt—not quite so sharp but still okay. By 1 P.M. you notice he's lost a shoe somewhere; and so you give him, along with some well-chosen words, his old yellow thongs. Then, around three, you substitute his old brown seersucker shorts for the navy ones, which got soaked in the sprinkler, and there goes your ball game. Absolutely no ensemble at all.

That is the story of most ensembles.

A lady, too, starts the season in a fair blaze of glory: a new beige silky gabardine suit, keyed to her last fall's alligator pumps and bag, a coffee-colored silk blouse, echoing doeskin gloves, and a truly hat-type hat which looked tremendous in the millinery department. (All millinery departments have patented mirrors which make you look three times better than you actually do, which explains some of the funny things you see on the streets.*)

Well, she wears her ensemble on a couple of occasions, and these are the times when she ought to run into her old beaux and never does.

Then, the next dress-up occasion, she doesn't want to wear the high-heeled alligator pumps because she's going to be standing all afternoon. So she wears her lower-heeled brown kid shoes, which leaves the alligator bag hanging in mid-air, so to speak, but it's full of her charga-plates and she hasn't time to change purses anyway, though she remembers to omit the hat which would look silly with the walking shoes.

Then, next time, she discovers that the coffee-colored blouse is at the cleaners, so she wears a paisley blouse which mysteriously throws the gloves out of gear and looks like the devil with the hat. But she has to wear the hat because her hair-dressing date isn't until tomorrow— And this, needless to say, is the day she *does* run into her old beaux, one per corner.

It must be admitted, however, that the ensemble system of dressing is the best one for the random-type dresser, because—once she assembles everything and puts it all where she can find it—she needn't think about it any more. People who know about these things tell me that it's the only way for her to insure having a well-turned-out look when she needs one. Keep certain things *together,* even if you have to keep them out of temptation's way, in your husband's office safe, and make sure you wear them with nothing else.

Now, a big thing with the fashion experts is the matter of dressing for your type. They don't consider the fact that some psyches are confused. You may be attuned to another era or tribe.

I know a lady who—if she could dress the way she'd really like to—would wear nothing but gypsy clothes: full swinging

---

* Should you ever come to, at home, with something unreturnable and absolutely wild on your head, you can explain that your old college roommate picked it up for you in Paris. A foreign pedigree helps many hats a great deal.

satin skirts, bare legs, high heels, bracelets to her armpits, and a sleazy chiffon blouse. But she knows as well as you do how fast she'd get kicked out of the P.T.A.

Or you may have a tweedy square-shouldered exterior and a chiffon soul, or vice versa. After all, who is purely one thing or another?

Well, there are several things you can do.

For instance, if you have the aforementioned Tarzan framework housing the soul of a lady poet, you can wear, over your tweed suit, a raincoat that's all flowers and frivolity.

You can hunt for—or have made for you—a severely tailored dress in a pretty feminine print.

You can divide your clothes neatly into outside tailored ones and inside frothy ones.

You can express the inner girl with all sorts of perfumes, colognes, and sachets. You can put bath salts into the last rinse water when you wash your underwear. You can even add cologne to the water you put in your steam iron! Isn't that a pretty thought?

In this matter of types, there is also another facet to be considered. The fashion experts are forever telling you to buy One Good Thing instead of two that are middlin' to piddlin'. But there again, they are assuming some assumptions that aren't necessarily so.

True, some people are happiest that way. They'll spend $60 for a simple straight black skirt, reveling in the hand-stitching or the imported wool or the label or whatever it is that's responsible for the $60 price tag. They'll take good care of it, too, and wear it for ten years. Dividing the price by ten, that comes to $6 a year, which—they consider—is fair enough.

But the in-between lady had better watch her step with this philosophy. It isn't always for her. In the first place, she doesn't usually take care of her clothes quite so well as she should. Also, she is apt to get hysterically sick of them (probably because she doesn't give too much profound thought to the ones she gets, and buys them more from impulse than plan). Therefore she's apt to want to kick herself when she remembers that $60, now long gone.

This brings us to the important matter of what items of apparel you can cheat on—that is, buy cheap * and get away with—and what items you can't.

I posed this question to several women whose style judgment I implicitly trust. The consensus was this:

WHAT YOU CAN CHEAT ON

1. *Summer shoes.* Throw them away at summer's end.
2. *Cocktail dresses,* especially bright ones. Just remove that awful rhinestone clip. It takes a trained eye to discern the difference between a flame-colored $22.95 number and a flame-colored $98.95 number, particularly after a couple of Gibsons.
3. *Formals.* Dance-floors are usually pretty dark.
4. *Jewelry,* if you choose carefully.
5. *Handbags,* ditto. This wasn't true a few years ago, but now the plastics people have improved their fake leathers to a truly amazing degree.
6. *Hats.*
7. *Underwear,* depending on your audience if any.
8. *Summer cottons or synthetic dresses.* Dispose of them at the end of the season because at that point the cheap ones have usually lost their bounce. If you don't dispose of them, you'll continue to wear them bounceless, and they'll look their price.
9. *Cosmetics,* depending on your personal needs.

WHAT YOU CAN'T CHEAT ON

1. *Girdles and bras,* unless you don't actually need to wear them anyway. If you do, the good ones are precisely engineered, and engineering doesn't come cheap.
2. *Shoes,* unless you wear them a dozen times only and throw them away. The trouble with cheap ones is that they lose their spurious good looks very rapidly but they won't quite fall apart, so you go on wearing them.

* It's unwise to buy *anything* cheap when you're feeling penniless, unless it's an astounding bargain, like a $159.00 dress for $9.95. Otherwise, when you wear your little cheapie, you'll just be reminded of how broke you are.

Speaking of bargains, the best way to tell if you really have one is to see if you enjoy wearing it without *telling* anybody it's a bargain.

3. *Belts.*
4. *Tailored suits, coats, dresses.*
5. *Anything made of alligator or lizard.*
6. *Nylon stockings.* Finding the right brand, size, gauge, and denier can take some doing; but once done, they look much better than the grocery type or factory seconds.
7. *Perfume.*
8. *Furs.*
9. *Gloves,* except for short white cottons.

Some women do very well, in this matter of cheating, by distracting the eye. They'll put an enormously expensive belt or pin or buckle on a plain $10.98 dress, and this fools new acquaintances nicely. They never suspect that the dress doesn't match the object in quality.

It doesn't fool your old acquaintances though. They just think, *That old thing again; isn't it a shame she can't buy herself some clothes.* However, they like you anyhow, and they're not going to tattle.

A few more pointers now, about shopping.

HOW TO BUY THINGS

Whenever possible, shop only when you feel cheerful.

To make sure you feel cheerful long enough to accomplish anything, wear comfortable shoes. But take a good big handbag along that will hold the shoes you plan to wear with whatever you buy.

Also, wear whatever underwear you'll be wearing with it—particularly the girdle and the bra. (If it's a snug-fitting dress, and you know you'll be wearing your Merry Widow with it, but don't want to be stuck with it or in it while you shop, put it in your big handbag too, and change in the fitting room.)

> "... *Balmain taught me everything. He said,* '*Always wear white gloves. It's best.*'"
> —QUEEN SIRIKIT OF THAILAND

When you are shopping for something, remember: if it is washable, you'll feel conscience-bound to wash it.

But, if it's expensive, you'll probably be afraid to wash it and—especially—iron it, even though it *is* washable. So don't let this point influence you too much.

HOW NOT TO BUY THINGS

When you are shopping with someone else and your own bank account is overdrawn, it's wise to wear a torn slip and a wilted bra. Then it will be easier not to try things on.

As a matter of fact, before we buy anything more, we'd better look over some of the things we already have.

Now, many women do a lot more for their clothes than their clothes do for them. They dry-clean and wash and iron them and hang them up neatly and air them and keep all the buttons sewed on, and still, when they put them on, nothing happens.

Should this be your problem, you should unload them.* A good way to do this is to have a rummage sale, none of the proceeds of which go to charity. (After all, you contribute to every worthy cause that comes along, don't you, and aren't you up to your clavicle in Campfire cookies?)

I belong to a little group of money-avid friends who, periodically, do this. Fortunately, we're all more or less the same size. So we assemble our closet dregs—things that are all right but have lost their *joie de vivre*, so far as we're concerned—pin a price tag on them for whatever we think the traffic will bear—and have an interesting evening's buying and selling. If you're lucky, you come home a little richer to a pleasantly bare closet.

And never forget the Goodwill Bag, or the Volunteers of America, or whatever other ways the community has developed for sharing the wealth. Be sure you put things into the bag soon enough for someone else to enjoy them. There is little demand now for Empress Eugénie hats.

Also, don't cut the buttons off, or remove the belt, as some scant-souled citizens have been known to do. Such conduct is unethical and lousy.

However, even though you've cleaned the closet of the

---

* Don't unload a too-short slip, though. You can cut the bottom off and use it as a camisole to prevent that peek-a-boo look when you're wearing sheer shirts with pants. Don't unload yellowed white shirts, either. You can easily dye them darker, to wear with jeans when you're plowing the north 40.

things you no longer wear, there will remain some things you'll have to take reasonable care of because you like them. Hence, some devastating data about closets.

A good thing to do is to cut notches in your closet clothes-pole, about three inches apart. This keeps suits and dresses from huddling together and wrinkling themselves.

Also, you can squeeze a wire coat-hanger up at both ends, so it is shaped like an idiot grin, then hang a slip or a night-gown on it. This keeps them from billowing out at you or sliding off the hook, whenever you open the closet door.

And the best way to hang up slacks or pants is by the cuffs, of course, upside down. (If you're short of regular pants-hangers, spring-type clothespins on regular wire hangers will work all right.) This shakes out wrinkles, and if they're your husband's pants, it might shake out a few dimes and nickels too.

It's also a good idea to hang up another shoebag somewhere (besides the one you keep your shoes in). This is for handy odds and ends like

> shoe polish
> shoe brushes
> clothes brush
> a small sewing kit (*if you don't have a Useful Box in your dressing room; see page 98*)
> cellophane tape
> Simonize lubricant (*if you have any alligator shoes or bags, they'll last longer if you treat them with it once in a while*)

You'll find the cellophane tape handy for many things— for instance, when you notice that the hem is coming out of a skirt, and you've neither the inclination nor the time to sew it. Just tape it down, and you'll look less as though you'd been dressed by the White Queen.

A roll of it is handy in your sewing box, by the way, if you have a sewing box. Tape down the thread ends of spools instead of trying to find those silly spool notches which have usually broken off anyway. Then things will be less of a tangle.

And it's a good lint remover or hair remover, if you have been sitting where a white poodle was. You must be conscientious and use a lot of tape, but it will do the job nicely.

For situations less drastic, a slightly dampened rubber sponge is all you need.

Also, should you ever make the mistake of buying a dress which has a basted-in linen collar, you must force yourself to rip out the basting and substitute snap-fasteners. Otherwise, the collar will nevermore be seen on the dress, after you've once taken it off to wash it.

However, in all these things, let us not be unduly conscientious. As the poet has put it so neatly:

> A sweet disorder in the dress
> Kindles, in clothes, a wantonness. . . .

In other words, absolute meticulousness is a little fearsome. Whereas, someone who is a bit rumpled looks as though she might be rumpled a bit more, and if you are in the mood or market for rumpling, it is just as well to keep this point in mind.

So, back to the shops, finally, where we come to one more problem which is often the lot of the in-between lady. *She is, unfortunately, given to compromise.*

For instance, she may feel, vaguely, that a princess-style dress becomes her. So—when she is shopping for something to wear (and usually this is for a specific and looming occasion)—she may well come home with a gold princess dress, even though gold always turns her the color of fresh asparagus. But she'll wear it philosophically, figuring that, after all, you can't have everything.

But sometimes you can. This fact was once pointed out to me by an unusually intelligent fashion editor, whose name I won't drop because that would be name-dropping.

She said that when you are uncertain what you look best in, and what to buy, do this:

Think back over your lifetime of clothes and select the three or four things that shine in your memory. (Into each life some truly euphoriant clothes must fall, if only through sheer accident.) Then try to pin down just what it was about each one that specifically warmed your heart.

Perhaps you'll come up with a list like this:
> the mandarin collar on a pair of pajamas
> the black velvet trim on a suit
> the houndstooth check of a jacket
> the peplum of a dress

Thus, you're a little clearer in your own mind what it is that you're subconsciously looking for.

Now, finding it would be a small miracle. But chances are good that you can find an able dressmaker—ask around, check the papers, advertise—who can incorporate two or three or even all these points into one suit or dress.

This, undoubtedly, would be your Fear Nothing costume: the clothes in which—you are cheerfully certain—you could go anywhere and do anything.

"A woman does not really need chic until the animal has lost some of its spring and the mind begins to prowl. This is the time for masking."   —AUTHOR UNKNOWN

II. MAKE-UP, HAIR, AND ALL THAT

"When life is too interesting to worry how my face looks, that's the way I like it."
    —JEAN VINT

The place to start is with a pink ceiling.

I know a lady who noticed that, through some curious combination of circumstances, she seemed to look a little older every year.

But she didn't waste time hunting magical creams. She had her husband paint her dressing room and bathroom ceilings a lovely soft rose. Also, she started wearing a little lipstick to bed—not enough to smear the pillowcase or anyone, just enough to minimize early-morning trauma.

Thus, with practically no work on her part, she looked immensely better to herself every time she looked in the mirror or put on her make-up, and she is now so mentally healthy she's almost unbearable.

She could have gone even further and tinted the ceilings in the dining room, living room, and hall, which would have made her guests look better too. Some guests need all the help they can get.

Incidentally, did you ever take a clear-eyed look at the ladies behind the counter who peddle those magical creams?

Not long ago I decided to get a jar of the latest queen-bee-juice-and-turtle-oil preparation, to banish those tiny tiny flaws the cosmetic people keep talking about. This royal preparation was royally priced, but I was nonetheless determined, until the saleslady told me she used it herself. She had a face like a well-oiled cowboy boot, and while it looked well-oiled, it didn't necessarily look any better. So I decided to leave her to her own tiny tiny flaws, and me to mine.

Anyway, there is always face-lifting, which is safe, simple, and painless these days, if you find a good surgeon to do it. Its average cost is a thousand dollars—not much more than the price of a bang-up vacation—and it lasts five to ten years. At the end of that time, you can have it redone, if you still care all that much.

It seems more sensible, therefore, to save up for a major crack and really get some results, instead of piddling away the dollars, jar by jar. So, when all the wee wisdoms in this chapter finally let me down with a resounding phhhlump— when things get totally out of hand instead of just semi— when I look for my face some morning and can't find it, this is what I aim to do.

I've noticed something else: if you conscientiously prepare and apply your face as the beauty people tell you to do— and I have tried this—you spend 900% more time at it than usual, but you look only 6% better.

This seems to me to be a poor return on the investment. So my tendency—a fairly general tendency too, I find—is to do the minimum, most of the time, and only rarely make the old hundred-dollar try.

For example, it's mildly true that make-up can make your nose and chin a little less prominent or a little more so, if you care to bother.

If you want one or both to recede, you use *darker* foundation on them, blending it with extreme care into the lighter foundation you use on the rest of your face. (This makes pouches under your eyes a little less noticeable too.)

If you want to bring things forward, you use *lighter* foundation on them, in the same careful time-consuming way. (If, instead of pouches, you occasionally have dark circles under your eyes, you'd use lighter foundation on them too, to make them match the rest of your face.)

Still, it's a lot of trouble, and it does you only about 6% worth of good frontways, and none at all from the side. The minute anyone sees your profile, the cat's out of the bag. So you'd hardly do it every morning—just on those occasions when you think every iota counts.

Noses can be altered surgically, of course. If it is far too big, you can have it bobbed. This operation has made many people happier and some of them prettier. And you can have a too-small nose built up, though I don't see why anyone should. *Cute as a button* has been standard English for a long time.

As for the chin, about all you can actually do is keep it clean.

The suggestions on skin, hair, legs, and so forth in this section will not include any six-per-centers which take any real doing or time; just six-per-centers which don't. (There is hardly a beauty hint in the world—except for a hair hint we'll come to presently—which nets you more than 6%, no matter what.)

Briefly, let's consider lipstick.

A good thing to bear in mind, in choosing the color, is the color of your teeth. The right shade of lipstick can make them look whiter. Teeth differ in their pigments. If yours tend toward the yellow-orange stripe of the spectrum, an orange-red lipstick will make them look more so. You might ask your dentist what color family your teeth belong to.

You can make lipstick stay on longer with an egg timer. Apply a thick coat of lipstick, blot it gently, powder over it, and turn the egg timer over. (You can make the bed or change the baby meanwhile, but no smoking or drinking.) When the three minutes are up, apply another coat and blot it again. This takes care of things for quite a spell.

Then, I know a girl with a beautiful mouth who always uses a *darker* shade of lipstick on her upper lip. She swears this does something or other.

Also, great numbers of people are devoted to lipstick brushes, which, they admit, take longer but achieve a clearer line.

Beauty experts are fond of saying you can reshape your mouth with lipstick, and if you are an expert, you probably can. At least, it works beautifully on their photographs of models. But it doesn't seem to work so well on real people. In any sort of a dim light you can see where they overshot or undershot their upper lips.

There is a psychoanalytical school, too, where lipstick is concerned. You can read a girl's character after a glance at how she wears down her lipstick:

> If it becomes worn on the bias, she will do anything for money.
>
> If it becomes blunt on the end, like a pencil eraser, she is extraordinarily interested in men.
>
> If it stays pointed clear to the end, she is or would be a wonderful mother.

A good thing to know about make-up in general is this: after applying your foundation and powder, wring out a washcloth in cold water and press it gently to your face for a moment. This gives you a not-quite-so-made-up look and it sets the powder.

Sometimes your face needs more of an assist than just make-up can give it. If you are catching a cold or had a swinging Saturday night, a big crisp white collar or a white scarf will make you look better than you feel.

If your skin is dry as a matzo, you may find that it helps to use moisturizer *every morning* on your face and neck before you apply your make-up. If it is only half as dry as a matzo, you can remedy the situation by washing it at night with cold cream, soap, and water all at once. Cold-cream your face thoroughly, then wash off the cold cream with a warm soapy washcloth and rinse it well.

Rinsing, by the way, is *big*. It's best to use a spang-clean washcloth right out of the linen closet for rinsing off the soap, because there will still be a little soap left in the other one. This makes for a lot of laundry but a softer face.

Evening Glamour

I read once, in some terribly authentic beauty article, that you can achieve an ethereal look at night by using a foundation cream and powder that are slightly lighter than the color you use in the daytime.

I tried this and was underwhelmed, but maybe it will do something for you.

If it doesn't, you can probably fix it up with rouge. The rouge should be the middle layer, between the foundation and the powder, so you can powder it to the tone you want. However, this means you'd have to start all over, and at this point your husband is probably chewing the carpet anyway. So just put a *wee* bit of rouge on top of what you already have, and nobody will mind.

Then there is eye make-up.

This is something you either take to naturally, like the French horn, or else you don't. Either way, it takes a lot of couth to wear it in the daytime, except for eyebrow pencil and a little mascara.

It takes a lot of time, too—blending the eyeshadow up and out, and powdering over it so it will stay, and then—hardest of all—using the eyeliner ever so carefully so it doesn't look like a child's crayonwork. (All this before you've even touched your lashes, you understand, or your eyebrows.)

If it makes you feel happy, you should wear it. If you do, choose your eyeshadow according to the color of your costume, if you're brown-eyed. (You could wear brown eye shadow, but it often makes people look liverish.) If you're blue-eyed or green-eyed, blue or green eyeshadow will tend to make your eyes infinitesimally more so.

Don't believe the people who say that eye make-up, properly applied, is undetectable, because they are telling you a taradiddle. There's no reason it should be undetectable, either, any more than lipstick is.

The thing about it is this, though: eye make-up always shows that you're trying hard, which may or may not be a good idea, depending on the circumstances.

I know a girl who makes a lot of distance with plain old vaseline. She rubs just a little on her eyelids and it gives her a moist, edible look.

Now, some girls apply make-up only to their faces and necks, but often the same foundation cream or pancake make-up they're using could do quite as much for their legs.

There is no point in putting sheer nylons on legs that are bumpy or scarred or marred with little broken veins. But any medium beige or rose face make-up will hide most of these and give the legs a nice glow into the bargain, under the stockings.

This is a good thing to do sometimes, even though your legs are fine and flawless, because it improves the color of washed-out nylons, should you be stuck with any.

Another thing: depilatory creams make legs smoother than shaving does, but they take longer.

And speaking of hair:

The biggest news about it is the big wig revival; and the big mistake the wig people have made is stressing the mad gay whimsy of it all.

So, when most women think *wigs,* they think *Copacabana and/or Racquet Club.* They think of being a ravishing red-head at lunchtime and a moon-glow blonde for the cocktail hour.

Admittedly, the idea has a certain pixie charm, but coming right down to cases, it would suit neither the philosophies, pocketbooks, nor husbands of most women I know.

However, if you own a wig that is an exact replica of your own hair, as it looks at its best, think of the practical advantages! For instance, you need a wig:

If you resent the money you spend at beauty salons. Your wig needs dry-cleaning only once every two months, even though you wear it every day (unless it is white or platinum, of course, and even in that case it would require less frequent attention than your own hair). You can do it yourself with dry-cleaning fluid, if you're good at setting hair. Or drop it off at a beauty shop that does this sort of work and have it cleaned, and restyled too, if you like.

If you are ham-handed, as I am, when it comes to doing your own hair, or if your life is too hectic to keep regular hairdressing dates. The wig will bridge that mussy period when things are out of hand.

If you swim a great deal. Just towel-dry your own hair, then put your wig on.

If you drive with the top down. Sometimes the wind-blown look is better on magazine covers than on people.

If you're sick in bed. You can have the morale-building effect of pretty hair without the bother.

If you're going broke with expensive tint jobs. The wig makers can duplicate *any* color.

If your life is subject to last-minute social emergencies.

If you like an intricate hair-style and your husband objects to pincurls and rollers.

If you're traveling abroad and don't want to be bothered.
You can get a good wig for about $100, which isn't much for such an enduring investment. (Though prices start at around $65, the cheaper ones are machine-tied, don't contain as much hair, and in general aren't quite so satisfactory.) And you can get one whether you live in mid-Manhattan or Charred Stump, Wyoming—any place where there is a beauty shop. In smaller communities, these are the contact and source of supply.

They're practically undetectable, of course. No one has ever asked me if I'm wearing a wig. People don't believe it even when you're perfectly frank. "I have to wash my wig tonight," you say, and no one thinks a thing about it.

So get one.

In the meanwhile, until it arrives, here are a few random suggestions about your own hair.

The eggtimer you used on page 139—for putting your lipstick on—is also helpful in brushing hair. Three minutes is a long time and you're apt to cheat, without the timer. But if you brush daily until all the sand is down, your hair will shine and your scalp will appreciate it too.

Now, if you can't set your own hair satisfactorily and would like to learn how, you might do as a friend of mine did.

She paid for the full morning's time of a hairdresser whose work she liked, having the hairdresser show her. The hairdresser put it up, while she watched, then took it down. Then *she* put it up, while the hairdresser watched and criticized, and took it down, and put it up again.

It was a grim morning's work, and it cost her about $15, I believe (though, in any case, this would vary with shops and operators). But my friend can do a fair job on herself now, and she considers the money well spent.

If you have trouble getting your hairdresser to do your hair as you like it, and then one day—through some fluke of circumstance—he gets it right, have someone take a close-up snapshot of you, quickly.

Then bring it in, whenever you visit the hairdresser's, and prop it prominently against the mirror, to remind him.

(This is also valuable in giving a new beauty operator something to aim at.)

Before we get to the business of perfume and diets and such, let us consider briefly the matter of

Hands

A woman once asked a famous beauty authority what she should do to have beautiful hands.

Said the beauty authority, who was honest as well as famous, "Nothing." By which he meant, of course, that work makes hands muscular, it usually enlarges the knuckles somewhat, and it subjects the skin to roughening and abrasions.

These are facts which the television commercials always overlook. They imply that even though your hands are kissed only by the family dog, this situation will change if you keep them properly lubricated.

But American men have never been much for hand-kissing anyway. And in Europe—even in Germany—the custom is on the skids, so you don't have to worry about *that*.

You needn't worry about muscles and knuckles either. Many intelligent people consider hands to be better-looking when they look as though they had done something: held a paintbrush or a golf club or a steering wheel or a baby or—in a word—something besides each other.

Somewhat rosy hands look less so with a rosy polish on the nails. But if the hands are quite red, it is best to use colorless nail polish, or sit on them.

The fast polish job is usually a poor excuse for a manicure, because the condition of the cuticle is a dead giveaway.

However, you can get by with the fast polish job if you keep your cuticle remover * and cotton swab by the bathtub and give yourself a one-minute treatment along with your bath. It helps, too, to get the habit of pushing back your cuticle every time you dry your hands. Then you're in shape to apply a swift coat of polish in the two minutes while you're waiting for the guests or the baby sitter.

You must remove it though—no matter how good it looks —when the evening is over. With only that one thin coat of polish, and no base coat or sealer, your manicure doesn't

---

* Olive oil is a good cuticle softener, though rather greasy.

have a prayer, and it will become patchy-looking in a hurry.

When you take time out to give yourself a good thorough manicure, it will last a day or two longer if you remove a hairline of polish at the tip of each nail. And if you can do so, wait a solid hour before you apply the final sealer coat.

Another thing: even though you prefer to do your own manicuring, it is helpful to have a professional job once in a while, if you know a really good manicurist. (There is a great difference between the expert and the average practitioner.) This gives you a fresh start which lasts for weeks.

THE 9 PLACES WHERE A WOMAN SHOULD WEAR PERFUME

At the bend of each elbow	2
On the pulse of each wrist	2
Behind each ear	2
On each eyebrow	2
At the base of your throat	1

Also, I know a girl who sprays her feet with cologne after she bathes and before she puts on her nylons.

And I know a charming Viennese girl who puts perfume in her mouth—touches it lightly to her gums with a finger tip. Talking to her is a mighty heady experience, believe me.

Now, if you'd like an all-of-a-pieceness that's above and beyond the call of duty, you can have hand lotion of the same scent as your favorite perfume, by making it yourself.

You go to the drugstore and ask for 2 drams of gum tragacanth (feeling a little sinister as you do this). You also buy 2 ounces of glycerine and as small a bottle as possible of bay rum.

When you get home, you soak the gum tragacanth overnight in half a pint of warm water.

In the morning, beat it with an eggbeater. Now add the 2 ounces of glycerine, 1 ounce of the bay rum, and half an ounce of this favorite perfume of yours.

Beat it again, and bottle it.

On the subject of dieting, millions of words have been printed and ignored about Asking Your Doctor, and the virtues of balanced exercise and diet, and so on. So in these pages we'll touch, instead, on a few approaches to the diet problem, and some small assorted facts.

For one thing, the random housewife often has a random figure, which tends to come and go. Sometimes it is wise to square up to this fact in a practical fashion, as did a friend of mine.

She is an off-and-on dieter, with a range of twenty-five pounds. She realized one day, in one of those moments of truth that we're all occasionally blessed with, that this situation would probably continue; that sometimes she would weigh 125 pounds and sometimes she would weigh 150 pounds.

So she acquired for herself a minimum wardrobe of good-looking 150-pound clothes, and now she doesn't worry about it so much. She knows that, in either case, she'll have something to wear.

It is a matter—as so many things are—of knowing yourself, and what you will or will not do. Some girls get good results with the carrot-in-front-of-the-nose technique. They'll buy a charming and reasonably expensive size 10—if that's the size they're aiming for—and hang it prominently in the bedroom, to keep them reminded.

But for other girls, this doesn't prove to be incentive enough. Finally the dress goes out of fashion, and they've merely spent all that money, and they feel miserable about it. You must know your own strength, and it is unwise to overestimate it.

One jellybean contains 7 calories.

You look somewhat thinner if your hairdo is reasonably sleek rather than bouffant.

Now, dieting being—as it so often is—a matter of mood, it is wise to keep some diet foods handy, for those mornings when you awaken with a surge of ambition and decide *this is the day*. If the dietetic fruits and salad dressing and the fatrecal are *there*, you can pin down your resolution with action, before it fades.

Never tell anyone you're on a diet.

If she is plumper than you are, she'll start talking you out of it. If she is thinner, it will bore her. If it's possible—that is, if you are dieting by merely cutting down on ordinary foods—keep it a secret even from the family. Otherwise you may have a feeling that they're secretly checking up on you, which can be infuriating. You'll find yourself taking on a load of chocolate caramels, just to show who's boss.

A female halibut usually weighs ten times more than her mate.

There are, of course, many ways to diet.

I know a woman who has kept the same weight and approximately the same figure for forty years, by means of a simple expedient. One day a week, she eats nothing at all. The other six days she eats normally, whatever she likes.

This cuts down her weekly caloric intake, you see, by approximately 1,800 calories. Figured yearly, that is 93,600.

The day she usually chooses is Monday, when she seldom goes out and when she's tired of the sight of food anyway, after the weekend cooking.

Of course, most people who go on a diet usually do so because they feel fat. It is convenient, however, if you feel fat and rich.

Then you can diet on fine expensive things like steaks, broiled rare, and luscious fresh fruits either in or out of season. The family will eat right along with you and not mind it a bit, which is an advantage truly worth saving up for. You don't have to prepare two meals.

When you are dieting earnestly, by the way, and inclined to feel melancholy sometimes as you think of the delicious calorie-laden things you'll never again be able to eat, you must realize that this is not so.

When you have finally lost that 30 pounds, your metabolism will have speeded up considerably, and you will be able to eat some lovely rich goodies without having them show, if you do so in moderation, of course, and take an occasional sounding, with the bathroom scale.

And speaking of bathroom scales: a grim fact we all must face is that you may well be heavier, even though your clothes still fit. Clothes—even as waistlines—stretch.

Then, too, your waist measurement may have increased, even though your weight hasn't. If this is the case, and you are determined to pare down a few inches through exercise, a good way to do it is this:

Encircle your waist with a cloth tape measure, pulling it comfortably snug—then mark your waist measurement with a colored crayon. Now sew snap-fasteners on the tape—the first one at the start of the tape and the second two inches slimmer than where the crayon mark is.

The tape will then be a good gauge of how you're doing. When you can finally snap the snap-fasteners, you're done.

All diet-minded people need one of the stickless greaseless frying pans to cook in.

Another good thing for them to have is this easy recipe for low-calorie Oven French Fries:

Set the oven for 475°.

Cut three raw potatoes in strips.

Drop them into a bowl containing one tablespoon of oil and one tablespoon of water mixed together. Stir the potato strips until they're well coated. Then bake them for half an hour in your 475° oven and serve them quite hot. This will serve four or five people, depending on how hard they're dieting.

One of the cheerier facts about dieting is that a one-and-a-quarter-mile walk, once a day, will fend off ten extra pounds a year, if you don't increase your grocery intake at the same time. (And there's no reason anyone should—that isn't a big enough hike to affect your appetite.)

It is interesting, too, for the random housewife to know how many calories she's spending per minute at her various projects around the house. This is how it goes:

ACTIVITY	CALORIE COST PER MINUTE
Sitting	1.11
Sitting & reading	1.11
Sitting & eating (*not counting what you eat*)	1.28
Sitting & playing cards	1.32
Resting in bed	0.93
Standing & staring	1.30
Standing & dusting	2.25
Personal toilet	1.73

Dressing	2.93
Taking a shower	2.93
Making the bed	4.20
Shining shoes	3.36
Mopping floors	4.15
Walking outdoors	4.89
Walking downstairs	6.06
Walking upstairs	15.92
Kneeling	1.00
Washing clothes	2.33

This is practical information to have, because you can use it to make room for more little treats while you're dieting. Like this, for example:

In our house, it is 16 steps to the second floor. To walk up and down them, at a moderate pace, takes me eighteen seconds and burns up approximately 7 calories. Therefore, if I would do this 15 times, it would burn up about 105 calories —or the exact calorie count of a one-inch square of fudge, or one pancake, or 5 slices of crisp bacon, which I could then eat, in all good conscience.

(Or I could make the bed twenty-four times, for about the same calorie count, but this sounds like a dreadful way to spend a morning.)

Finally, now, to the matter of preserving yourself for posterity, or what to do when you're having a picture taken.

What most of us are after, when we have a picture taken, is a good natural-looking picture that doesn't resemble us. To achieve this, these are good points to bear in mind:

1. When it is to be a full-figure snapshot or portrait, your figure won't look so full if you will twist a little.

Like this: First, stand squarely facing the camera. Then put your right foot behind your left foot, and twist your body toward the foot that's behind. Make sure you straighten your shoulders and hold your chin and rib cage high. You will look slimmer this way, and more graceful too. In fact, you can stand like this whenever you want to look especially fetching, whether you're having a picture taken or not.

2. If you like perfume, wear a little. It has a good psychological effect on you as you pose.

3. Wear pale blue, or tan, or green, or something of about that color intensity, rather than black or white.

4. Don't wear a hat, because no matter how smart the hat is now, posterity will snicker.

5. If smiling comes at all naturally to you, it is better to smile than not to. It is true that when you've been standing or sitting for aeons, waiting for the photographer to do something, there seems little to smile about. Therefore, it's helpful to remember that words with long or short E or I sounds make you look agreeable. (If you give a long drawn-out mooooo as the photographer presses the button, you will look singularly affectionate, which is a good thing to remember if you're sending this picture overseas.)

Cheese is, of course, a good word to say, and so is *whisky*. A good sentence to repeat, over and over, enunciating each syllable with clarity, is: "I believe I merit cheese and whisky."

And, at this point, you probably do.

12: The Hostess with the Leastest

*"Fan the sinking flame of hilarity
with the wing of friendship, and
pass the rosy wine!"*

—DICK SWIVELLER

GIVING A PARTY is often—as so many things are—a matter of timing.

One of the best times to give a party, or so a friend of mine feels, is when the house is torn up. When the painters are busily painting and the plumbers plumbing, your guests can't expect much of you. They feel it's lucky you even found the whisky, let alone an ice cube to drop into it, and you're also credited with valor under terribly adverse circumstances.

Though few people remodel often enough to handle all their social obligations in this fashion, it is a good thing to do whenever possible. Otherwise, the freewheeling housewife—full of vague unease anyway when guests are expected—tends to turn into a compulsive ceiling-sweeper and mantel-duster. She becomes immensely aware of things she hasn't done that she probably should have, like vacuuming the hot-air registers and dusting the old cans of peas on the far right end of the top shelf of the pantry. Unless the house is in a pleasant state of excusable chaos—in which case nothing makes any difference anyway—she is apt to wear herself out with these chores, at a time when simply getting the food and drink ready is trouble enough.

Then there are other approaches.

I also know a lady who depends heavily on candlelight. Not just at the dinner table, mind you, but everywhere. She has some lovely old wall sconces which take candles, and some beautiful candelabra and a collection of quaint candlesticks. When you go to her house for dinner, you'd think she'd never heard of Thomas A. Edison. Not only does the house look most attractive, lit in this fashion, but she needs to do little if any pre-house cleaning; for you can't see into the corners, or indeed, more than three feet ahead.

Actually, the important thing to remember to clean, before guests arrive, is the telephone. Telephones get an intimate, grimy look which is immediately noticed by guests, but not by hosts, who are used to it.

And you know how often the telephone is used at a party—to check babysitters or call taxis or—depending on how good the party is—to say Hiya booper ole socks to somebody's old college chum in Akron, Ohio.

However, the comforting fact is—and let's never forget it—people *huddle*. In a 40-by-50 living room, large enough to park four Cadillacs without dimpling a fender, eight guests will congregate and stay congregated in an area 10 feet square. It is the gravitational force of mutual attraction—the same force that keeps planets spinning, tides surging, sputniks circling, and holds the universe together. Newton's law will have to be repealed before people will scatter in a large room.

So don't clean up everywhere else.

A good thing for the freewheeling (or somewhat nervous) hostess to remember is the merits of drinking a jigger of ordinary salad oil before the people come. The combination of nerves and cocktails can sometimes prove distressing, and the oil will help prevent overdependence on aspirin, jellied consommé, B-1 pills, and black coffee, the following morning.

If you can't find the icebag, you can make one, of sorts, by filling a rubber glove with cracked ice and tying the wrist tightly.

In prettying up the table or tables, a good thing to know about is paraffin. When your flowers are heavy and your bowl is not, pour a puddle of paraffin into the bowl and, while it is still warm, set the flower frog in place.

However, the big thing to keep in mind—no matter how repellent the idea seems at first—is the advantages of giving *two* dinner parties, on *two successive nights*.

Giving only one dinner at a time is like having only one tonsil out at a time. You have all the pain twice, not to mention the trouble and expense. (Little consideration will be given to expense in this chapter, by the way, because if you ever stopped to figure out what a party cost, you wouldn't give it. We'll just mention in passing that you can give two dinners for the price of one and a half, because of the odds and ends. The flowers, if you went that far, the chicory, endive, raw mushrooms, outsize pecans, et cetera, all of which probably weren't used up the first night.)

But the main thing you save is trouble—the driveway swept, the wax fruit * dusted, the entree made.

When you give two dinners, on successive nights, pay careful attention to whom you invite and when. You should have the Maddengays on the *first* night, when there is a little more

---

* Wax fruit that looks like fruit is non-U, but if it's made of velvet or rattan or alabaster so it can't possibly fool anybody, it's okay. In any case, remember to remove the price tags before putting it in the pretty brass bowl.

And, if you should be using real fruit, line the pretty brass bowl with saran wrap first, or the fruit will do the brass no good at all.

sparkle in the soda, so to speak. Save the Oldenpooheds for the second, inasmuch as that is how you'll be feeling when this ghastly weekend is finally over. But it will be well worth it, when you consider those obligations so thoroughly taken care of.

Therefore, the four dinners which are starred in this chapter—and we will presently get to them—have been planned with this repeat performance in mind. The entrees, that is, can easily be made in double quantities all at once, without anyone's suspecting (as even your simpler-minded friends would if you served them a six-rib roast with some of the ribs gone).

A word about aprons.

If the usual kind offends your sense of the fitness of things, you might be happier in a Japanese happi coat, from some importer's shop. Or one of those white French smock affairs you find in small ads in exclusive magazines—which cover you up and make you look quite knowledgeable too.

Also, a big solid-colored bath towel, safety-pinned like a half-sarong, looks smarter than you'd think it would.

Or you can buy a springy, curved plastic towel rod at the dimestore (made to semi-encircle the waist), plus a few yards of striped sateen, denim, or toile de joie, and make yourself an apron wardrobe. Hem a piece the size of a kitchen hand towel, making one long-ways hem wide enough for the rod to go through. These are easy to wash and iron.

But, to put things in their logical order, let's first briefly consider the matter of drinks.

EVOLUTION

How perfect the tang of the tawny Martini,
  The first of the night, a delight to the brim!
How suave is the olive, serene at the bottom,
  The sliver of lemon that's riding the rim!

How beamish our host, coming in with the second!
  (He proudly constructs them himself, and we love it.)
How shrewdly those subtle proportions were reckoned!
  . . . If this time he bypassed the lemon, what of it?

How merry the guests, and hooray for the third!

Talk taxable income and sorrow who dares.
How cunning the medley—divine is the word!
. . . Though he seems to be fresh out of olives, who cares?

How frabjous the evening, as cometh the fourth!
Hail, prosit, and skoal! Let the party begin!
How tiresome, in truth, was that silly vermouth!
How crystalline-clear now, how virgin the gin!

This is one trouble with the ever-level pitcher of Martinis. It is too easy to fix, and the host—carried away with his genial role—is apt to keep refilling the glasses of his guests until their scuppers are awash. (Many a wife has noticed in pretty amazement how her husband—sluggish as he may be about fetching her a glass of water, any cozy evening at home—leaps to his feet with glad cries and fast replenishments whenever he sees a cocktail glass less than three-quarters full.)

I know a lady who discovered that her husband was a little less anxious to build another pitcherful, so promptly, if they were serving Daiquiris.* (Crushing the ice and squeezing the lime juice takes more doing than spattering vermouth, and for this reason she won't allow bottled lime juice in the house.) So, in that split-second while he hesitates, she announces dinner.

There's many another cocktail that would serve the same purpose, of course. Just make sure you have a bottle of bourbon or Scotch around, if Chuck is coming. You know how old Chuck is.

It is a thoughtful move, incidentally, to give your guests a little warning as to how much alcohol the evening is going to involve.

The thirsty guest who is apt to take one more cocktail than he actually needs, just for insurance purposes, may slow down a bit if you mention the amusing little Chablis you

---

* For 8 drinks they use the juice of 4 limes, 1½ ounces of finely granulated sugar, and 1½ cups of light rum. Shake—strain—pour.

Limes keep much longer, by the way, in a tightly closed jar in the refrigerator. This is good to remember at gin-and-tonic time.

Furthermore, limes are good for hiccups. Sprinkle a couple of drops of Angostura bitters on a lime quarter (or lemon) and take six swift sucks.

were lucky enough to find, or the fact that Irish Coffee is coming at him later.

Speaking of all this, it's an odd fact but a true one that alcohol's alcohol, no matter where you find it. A 1½-ounce jigger of whisky and an average 3½-ounce glass of sherry and a bottle of 4½% beer all contain about the same amount of alcohol. (Accordingly, some people who think they are coasting aren't really.) Also, it takes an hour and twenty minutes for all the alcohol from one drink to leave the body—a fact that so many hosts won't pay any mind to.

Another thing: you feel the effects of a drink more quickly when the liquor is mixed with soda rather than plain water. The bubbles carry the message a little faster.

When you ask a guest whether he prefers water or soda, and he hesitates or says, "Oh, either one," he really wants soda. He's just being tactful, you see—afraid the soda's too much trouble, or you don't have a bottle open. If he really prefers water, though, he'll say, promptly, "Water."

Some people are distressed because their olives lose their shine, once they get out of the bottle. But their olives would stay shiny if they'd add two tablespoons of vegetable oil to the liquid in the olive jar.

Should you ever care to make your own after-dinner brandy, by the way, you may do so. Fill a pint Mason jar a third of the way up with raisins. Then fill the jar with bourbon or rye whisky, and let it set for a week.

It has a nice fruity flavor, and the raisins are tremendous later in spice cake or fruitcake.

But now for the matter of food, which we'll approach in a roundabout way with two easy canapé recipes.

You can soak dried shrimp in sherry for four hours, and serve them on cocktail crackers.

Or, if you have a chafing dish to keep them hot in, and even if you don't, you can make

LITTLE ROUND CHINESE MEAT BALLS

You mix this together:
1 tablespoon powdered ginger
1½ pounds ground beef
1 crushed garlic clove
½ cup soy sauce
¼ cup water

Then you make little balls, about an inch in diameter, put

them in a roasting pan, and bake uncovered, for an hour, at 275°. Serve them with 50 toothpicks, because it makes 50 meatballs, or more than enough for the six or eight people we're serving in most of the following dinners.

A lazy susan for toads has been constructed at the University of Connecticut, because toads won't touch food that isn't moving. The toads sit near the rim of the apparatus and flick off bits of hamburger as it goes around.

Now, just a word, before we get to the menus and the recipes.

These have been evolved with buffet service in mind, but with prearranged places where the guests may sit. This is more comfortable, and allows for salad plates too, when it's indicated, instead of having one big sloppy plateful with the salad dressing running into the meat.

It makes no difference what places are prearranged, just so they are: TV tables, end tables, kitchen counters, or card tables. If it's card tables, you might have some round composition-board tops made, sometime, to set on top of them for occasions like this. You can then use round cloths and get rid of that classic card-table look.

About the cooking itself: there's hardly a dish that objects to being interrupted when it's two thirds done cooking. It's usually better to finish the cooking just before serving than to have cooked it completely and then reheat it.

And a word about desserts: In a former book of mine,* which was wholly concerned with the unpleasant subject of cooking, I earnestly recommended skipping the whole matter of desserts except for Irish Coffee and/or Oddments (mints, little cakes, sugared nuts, et cetera). I cannot now, with truth or honor, contradict myself. My heart leaps down when I behold a hostess coming my way with a Set Piece— a big fat cake or something flaming. I know if I don't eat it, her eyes will start to fill, and if I do eat it, I'll wish I hadn't. It seems to me unfair to place anyone on the sharp horns of this particular dilemma.

In my estimation, *petits fours* and truffle mints have never been surpassed, because the lucky guest can nibble or not,

* *The I Hate to Cook Book,* Harcourt, Brace & World, Inc., 1960; paperback, Crest Books, 1965.

as he prefers, and the lucky hostess didn't have to do any work on that particular department of the dinner.

In these menus, this is to be kept in mind. The dessert recipes that *are* included are there for the occasions when you know your guests are dessert people (and it is unfortunately true that some are). None of them is hard to make, and I don't see how any of them could let you down.

Here, then, are ten menus for those times when you are expected to go to more trouble than you ordinarily do, with the pertinent recipes included. None of the menus is in the least formal, and none has any hidden landmines to trip over. Each tastes good, too, and is—in the words of the contractor who recently expanded our front porch—good enough fer who it's fer.

✳ Menu 1
MORE-OR-LESS MEDITERRANEAN DINNER
Manny's Lamb Stew
Syrian Pecan Salad
Hot Rolls or Biscuits
Harem Cream

MANNY'S LAMB STEW
serves 6-8

(This is quite a good lamb stew because it contains no peas of any description, and it's made with lemon juice instead of white wine. You could use white wine, but you might as well save it to drink with the dinner.

If you are following the rollicking suggestion given earlier, and having two dinners in a row, double this and do everything up to adding the carrots and potatoes. Then do that, half an hour before serving time, each evening.)

2½ pounds lean stewing   1 crumbled bay leaf
   lamb * cut in edible-size
   pieces

* Lamb shoulder is good. Get the butcher to bone and cut it for you, and make sure he trims the fat off.

4 tablespoons olive oil
1 good-sized onion, peeled and chopped
1 clove garlic, crushed
2 tablespoons flour
1½ cups chicken consommé (canned, instant powdered, or cubes)
1½ teaspoons salt
¼ teaspoon pepper

¼ teaspoon marjoram
1 ounce lemon juice (2 tablespoons)
1-pound can small white onions
4 carrots, scraped and cut in chunks
4 medium potatoes, peeled and cut in pieces
1½ tablespoons finely chopped parsley

Brown the lamb in the olive oil, using a heavy skillet with a lid. Then remove the lamb and pour out most of the oil, leaving only enough to sauté the onion and garlic in it. Do that.

Now put the lamb back in, sprinkle it with the flour, and add the consommé, salt, pepper, bay leaf, marjoram, and lemon juice. Stir it thoroughly, then put the lid on the skillet and simmer it all for half an hour. (Skim off the fat now, if it seems to need it, though it won't if the butcher did a good job.) Twenty-five minutes before you serve it, add the onions, carrots, and potatoes. Finally, sprinkle the parsley on top.

SYRIAN PECAN SALAD
serves 8

Get 2 pounds of fresh spinach and wash it if you have to (see page 51). Then you'll need:

1½ teaspoons salt
8 to 10 green onions, using part of the green too
4 tablespoons olive oil
4 tablespoons lemon juice
¾ cup chopped salted pecans

Chop the spinach coarsely, in mouth-size pieces. Sprinkle it with the salt, then muss it with your hands, squeezing the salt into it. This creates some green juice, so squeeze it dry. Then add the sliced onions (and at this point you can let it set in the refrigerator, several hours if you like). When dinner is ready, add the olive oil, lemon juice, and pecans, toss it, and serve.

HOT ROLLS

Get bakery ones, or refrigerated ones.

If you'd rather serve biscuits, roll the dough out twice as thin as usual, butter it all, and fold it over once—then cut. Then they'll split open handily and look quite polite.

HAREM CREAM
makes 2 ice-cube trays full;
serves 10 to 12

2 cups whipping cream	¼ cup chopped candied
2 12-ounce cans apricot nectar	ginger
4 tablespoons lemon juice	slivered toasted almonds
½ cup sugar	(*buy them by the can*)

Whip the cream till it's stiff, then add everything but the almonds. Remove the dividers from your two ice-cube trays, and pour the mixture into the trays, and set them in the freezing compartment.

When it's mushy—you might look in about an hour, and if it isn't mushy then, it won't be long—pour it into a bowl and beat it thoroughly with a tablespoon till it's smooth. Then replace in trays and freeze until firm.

When you serve it, scoop it out like ice cream and sprinkle the slivered toasted almonds on top.

✳ Menu 2
AMIABLE CURRY DINNER
serves 6
Amiable Chicken Curry
Plain White Rice
Sambals
Green Salad with Oil-and-Vinegar Dressing
Beer

N.B. Inasmuch as beer is good with this dinner, your predinner cocktail might be a Dog's Nose: 1½ ounces gin added to 8 ounces of chilled beer. No ice.

AMIABLE CHICKEN CURRY

(This is a nice co-operative curry which will wait for hours, if it has to, in the top of a double boiler, and it's

easy to double. Also, you don't have to stew a whole chicken to get the meat. The 2 tablespoons of curry powder listed here are enough for most people, but if you're exceptionally curry-minded, add another.)

4 whole chicken breasts	an onion, chopped
2 cans cream of chicken soup	an apple, chopped
2 tablespoons curry powder	4 tablespoons butter
a little milk if you need it, preferably condensed	

Simmer the chicken in about one and a half cups of water until it's tender. Remove the meat and chunk it, but don't throw out the water.

Now melt the butter, add the curry powder, chopped apple and onion, and sauté fifteen minutes. Then stir in the undiluted soup, thinning it with the water you cooked the chicken in, and a little milk if you need it, till it's a good sauce consistency. Add the chicken and keep it all hot in the top of your double boiler.

SAMBALS

Use three or four of any of these, depending on how much you feel like chopping, and how many little dishes you have:

chopped peanuts	chopped crisp bacon
chopped green onions	chopped cucumber
sliced bananas (*with a bit of*	raisins
lemon juice sprinkled on	coconut
them to prevent their	chutney
discoloring)	mustard pickle *

* Menu 3
END-OF-THE-MONTH DINNER
serves 8
1000 Beans and a Meatball †
Coleslaw
(*with chopped cucumbers and green onions added*)

---

* This sounds odd but tastes good, and some people think no curry is curry without it.

† When doubled, this is called *2000 Beans and 2 Meatballs.*

French Bread

Sugared Pineapple   Thin Sugar Cookies

N.B. This dinner is good, easy, and cheap, even though you buy the French bread, coleslaw, and slice-and-bake cookies. Fix the pineapple the night before so it has time to get thoroughly sweet.

1000 BEANS AND A MEATBALL

In a big casserole mix:

1 package frozen lima beans, thawed enough to separate
5 cups drained kidney beans
6 cups baked beans, New England type
1 tablespoon dry mustard
¼ cup brown sugar
2 teaspoons salt
½ teaspoon pepper

Bake it forty-five minutes at 400°. While it's baking, make sixteen or twenty meatballs out of

2 pounds ground beef
1 tablespoon salt
½ teaspoon pepper
1 small minced onion
¼ cup water

Brown them quickly in a little oil, then add

1 cup catsup
2 tablespoons vinegar
1 tablespoon brown sugar
½ teaspoon dry mustard
1 tablespoon butter

and simmer this, with the meatballs, for twenty minutes. Now put the meatballs and a can of drained small white onions on top of the beans, spoon the sauce on, and cook fifteen minutes at 400°.

✳ Menu 4
1ST-CABIN FRIDAY DINNER
Lucienne's Spinach-with-Crab ✳
Crisscross Potatoes
Simple Salad
Lemon Cake-Top Pudding

✳ If you're doubling this, put it in two casseroles, and keep one in the refrigerator until the next day.

LUCIENNE'S SPINACH-WITH-CRAB
serves 6

2 boxes frozen chopped spinach	1 tablespoon lemon juice
	nutmeg
½ pound grated sharp Cheddar	2 tablespoons butter
	2 tablespoons flour
1 pound crabmeat	1 can condensed tomato soup
1 tablespoon minced onion	1 cup sour cream

Cook the spinach till it's half done, then drain it well by pressing it with great firmness into a colander. Now put it in the bottom of a greased casserole dish, and sprinkle it with half the cheese, then with the crabmeat, minced onion, lemon juice, a dash of nutmeg—then the rest of the cheese.

Now melt the butter, blend in the flour, add the soup and simmer till slightly thickened. Cool it a little, stir in the sour cream, then pour it over the crab and cheese mixture, dot it with butter, and bake it *uncovered* in a 350° oven for thirty minutes.

CRISSCROSS POTATOES

Cut scrubbed, unpeeled baking potatoes in half the long way. With a knife, score the cut sides crisscross fashion, about a quarter-inch deep. Mix a little salt and dry mustard with butter—about a tablespoon of butter per potato-half—and spread this on the potatoes. Bake for an hour at 350°.

That's the same temperature the crab dish wants, so put the potatoes in a half-hour earlier.

SIMPLE SALAD

On salad plates arrange romaine, chicory, endive, or whatever you have. On top, arrange pretty green pepper rings, onion rings, and tomato slices. Over everything, drizzle oil-and-vinegar dressing.

LEMON CAKE-TOP PUDDING

Get the ready-mix kind and follow the crystal-clear directions on the box.

Menu 5
2ND-CABIN FRIDAY DINNER
Sesame Sole *

* Or halibut.

Tomato Aspic Salad *
Rolls
Saratoga Torte

SESAME SOLE

You need two pounds of fish. (If you're using halibut, it may come in one-pound pieces. If it's sole, four or six smaller pieces will be fine.)

First, toast: 2 cups soft bread crumbs
2 tablespoons sesame seeds

Then, into these, mix

½ teaspoon salt   3 tablespoons melted butter
½ teaspoon ground thyme   3 tablespoons water
⅛ teaspoon black pepper   ½ clove garlic, crushed

Salt and pepper both sides of the fish and give them a good squirt of lemon juice. Put stuffing on one slice of fish, put the other slice on top, dot with butter, and bake uncovered at 350° for thirty to forty minutes.

SARATOGA TORTE

(*This is easy, chewy, and good, and looks as though you'd gone to a lot of trouble. You can make it far in advance, too.*)

3 egg whites   14 two-inch-by-two-inch soda
1 cup sugar   crackers, coarsely crumbled
1 teaspoon vanilla   ¾ cup chopped walnuts
1 teaspoon baking powder   1 cup heavy cream

Beat the egg whites till practically stiff and then gradually add the sugar. Combine the crumbled crackers, walnuts, and baking powder, and fold them into the egg mixture along with the vanilla. Spread it in a nine-inch pie pan and bake at 350° for forty-five minutes. When it's cool, spread it with slightly sweetened whipped cream and refrigerate it at least two hours before you serve it. Grate a little baking chocolate on top, if you like, to give it more expression.

Menu 6
BLACK FOREST BEEF DINNER
Black Forest Beef and Onions

* I don't like tomato aspic myself, but if you do, I defend to the death your right to prepare it. This would be a good place for it if you want it and if you have a recipe. Otherwise, any tomato salad is quite all right.

Mashed Potatoes
Very Artistic Salad Plate
Oddments
N.B. For another touch of the Schwarzwald, serve beer.

BLACK FOREST BEEF AND ONIONS
(This is actually a stew, heavy on the onions.)
3 pounds beef chuck, in 1½-inch chunks
8 tablespoons butter *(but you don't use it all at once)*
¼ cup flour

¼ cup chopped parsley	6 onions, sliced
1 teaspoon thyme	1 teaspoon sugar
1 bay leaf, crumbled	1 teaspoon salt
2 tablespoons wine vinegar	½ teaspoon black pepper

2 or more cups beer

Put the flour in a paper bag, drop the beef chunks in after it, and shake. Then brown them in four tablespoons of your butter, in a deep skillet with a lid.

Then add everything from parsley through beer, in the list up there, and if the beer doesn't cover the meat, add a little more. Bring it barely to a boil, then simmer it for an hour, covered. Keep adding beer if you need to, for a nice stew effect. You can always drink what you don't put in the skillet.

Now sauté the onions in the rest of the butter, add the sugar, and cook till the onions, too, have a glazed look. Then add them to the beef and cook for fifteen minutes, or till the beef is tender.

I know a very good cook who says that most meat recipes calling for wine taste equally good made with beer.

MASHED POTATOES
Make the instant kind, adding plenty of butter and cream so they'll taste like mashed potatoes.

VERY ARTISTIC SALAD PLATE
Get a reasonable-sized can each of:

julienne beets	asparagus
julienne carrots	artichoke hearts
celery hearts	

Marinate them *separately* in bowls of oil-and-vinegar dressing (that is so the colors won't run). Then arrange them tidily on a bed of lettuce on a *big* plate: the asparagus and julienne vegetables spotted here and there like stacks of cordwood, the other things in neat clumps.

In the middle of the plate, put a bowl of Roquefort or Blue Cheese dressing.

Either beat mayonnaise, sour cream, and Blue Cheese till it tastes the way you want it to;

Or you can make this Blue Cheese dressing, which has a slight additional caramba because of the onion juice:

Beat together:

1 cup oil	½ teaspoon dry mustard
1 teaspoon salt	lots of pepper
2 teaspoons paprika	⅓ cup vinegar (*including a*
1 teaspoon onion juice	*little garlic vinegar*)

2 or 3 ounces Blue Cheese

Menu 7
GOOD DEPENDABLE HAM DINNER

N.B. Many hostesses automatically think *Baked Ham* when they are having a buffet, and many guests automatically think *Oh dear* when they get there and discover that's what they'll be eating.

They needn't be so fussy though. Many people in this world would jump at a good thick hot rosy slice of ham, and if your guests don't, they can major in the Green-and-White Casserole and the Curried Fruit, which leaves you more ham for the weeks ahead. Or in the Add-a-Pound Cake, which is heavy enough to sink a battle cruiser, though it's very good, and some people *like* things like this.

A big precooked preboned Canned Ham
Curried Fruit
Green-and-White Casserole
Hot Cornbread
Add-a-Pound Cake

Heat the ham according to the directions on the can.

CURRIED FRUIT

You need one number-two can each of apricots, pineapple, and pears. Put the juice (except for the pear juice, which you can throw out) in a saucepan, add a tablespoon of curry powder, and cook it down a little.

When the ham is half hot, pour off all the fat. Then place the fruit around it, and baste both the ham and the fruit with the sauce, occasionally, until the ham is ready.

Arrange the fruit around the ham, on the platter.

GREEN-AND-WHITE CASSEROLE
serves 8

2 packages frozen peas, cooked and cooled	1 teaspoon salt
	1 cup diced celery
3 cups cooked rice	¾ cup mayonnaise
1 middle-sized onion, finely diced (*or a bunch of green onions*)	1 cup buttered bread crumbs

Mix all this together. Put some more bread crumbs on the top, and bake uncovered, for an hour, at 350°.

HOT CORNBREAD
Use a mix, for heaven's sake.

ADD-A-POUND CAKE
Bake a ready-mix pound cake according to directions. When it's cold, slice it four times horizontally (as you'd slice bread for a sandwich loaf).

Now melt a package of chocolate bits in the top of the double boiler. Let it cool a bit, then mix it thoroughly with one cup of sour cream. Frost the layers like a cake, stack them, frost the outside, and chill. You should do this the day before.

Menu 8
YE OLDE CLASSICKE FRIED-CHICKEN DINNER

N.B. People tend to look down on Fried Chicken, but it has many advantages: you know how to fix it, it is inexpensive, and nearly everyone eats it. This menu is a good one, particularly if you number any children among your guests. The adults may think *Ho-hum* when they see the chicken, but they will probably find the 56th Street Walnut Rice quite interesting.

Ye Olde Classicke Fried Chicken
Newly Minted Peas
56th Street Walnut Rice
Any Dessert you like, or none

Fry the chicken the way you always do, or broil it, as on page 65.

To garnish the platter, put a number of peach halves—depending on how many people you are feeding—in a separate pan, and bake them for half an hour at 350°. Then fill them with chutney, and they'll look sprightly around the chicken, and taste good too.

NEWLY MINTED PEAS

Cook two packages frozen peas according to directions. Then add

  1 teaspoon sugar
  butter as you usually do
  1 teaspoon dried mint (*put it in the palm of your hand and bruise it gently to bring out the flavor*)
  salt, pepper

Mix it all together and serve.

56TH STREET WALNUT RICE
serves 6

3 cups cooked rice
⅓ to ½ cup coarsely chopped walnuts

6 tablespoons butter
2 tablespoons Worcestershire sauce

Melt the butter. Then add the Worcestershire. Add the nuts and brown them. If you prefer the nuts crisp, take them out now, drain them on a paper towel, and add them at the last minute. If not, mix everything together, keep it in a double boiler till serving time, and then put it in a hot serving dish.

And now for

Menu 9 *
DEEP-SEA SPAGHETTI DINNER
serves 6

Clam Spaghetti

French Bread   Red Wine

Green Salad with Tomatoes

Honeydew Melon with a scoop of Lime Sherbet

(*or lime sherbet drizzled with crème
de menthe if it isn't melon time*)

CLAM SPAGHETTI

Start the spaghetti cooking. Then cook the onion and garlic in oil and butter till they're light-colored. Add all the clam juice from the two cans of clams and simmer it for five minutes. Then add the clams and parsley, bring it barely to a boil (but don't let the clams really boil or they'll be tough).

Then mix it with the cooked spaghetti and add the Parmesan.

And that's *it*.

That's it. And it was a nice party, really. All nine of them. Or two of them. Or one of them.

And one of these days you'll put the house back together again. In your own random fashion, that is. Which works pretty well for you, at that, when all's said and done. (Though when *is* all ever said and done?) And, of putting houses back together again, there is no end.

Yes, one of these days.

But not now.

Not tonight . . .

ON A DEAD HOSTESS
*"Of this bad world the loveliest and best
Has smiled and said 'Good Night,' and gone to rest."*
—HILAIRE BELLOC

"Don't do like I do, do like
I *say* do."
—SOMEBODY'S GRANDMA

* There were going to be ten, but I got tired.

Index